Understanding
A Raisin
in the Sun

The Greenwood Press "Literature in Context" Series

Understanding *The Scarlet Letter*: A Student Casebook to Issues, Sources, and Historical Documents
Claudia Durst Johnson

Understanding *Adventures of Huckleberry Finn*: A Student Casebook to Issues, Sources, and Historical Documents
Claudia Durst Johnson

Understanding *Macbeth*: A Student Casebook to Issues, Sources, and Historical Documents
Faith Nostbakken

Understanding *Of Mice and Men, The Red Pony*, and *The Pearl*: A Student Casebook to Issues, Sources, and Historical Documents
Claudia Durst Johnson

Understanding Anne Frank's *The Diary of a Young Girl*: A Student Casebook to Issues, Sources, and Historical Documents
Hedda Rosner Kopf

Understanding *Pride and Prejudice*: A Student Casebook to Issues, Sources, and Historical Documents
Debra Teachman

Understanding *The Red Badge of Courage*: A Student Casebook to Issues, Sources, and Historical Documents
Claudia Durst Johnson

Understanding Richard Wright's *Black Boy*: A Student Casebook to Issues, Sources, and Historical Documents
Robert Felgar

Understanding *I Know Why the Caged Bird Sings*: A Student Casebook to Issues, Sources, and Historical Documents
Joanne Megna-Wallace

Understanding *The Crucible*: A Student Casebook to Issues, Sources, and Historical Documents
Claudia Durst Johnson and Vernon E. Johnson

Understanding *A Tale of Two Cities*: A Student Casebook to Issues, Sources, and Historical Documents
George Newlin

Understanding Shakespeare's *Julius Caesar*: A Student Casebook to Issues, Sources, and Historical Documents
Thomas Derrick

UNDERSTANDING
A Raisin in the Sun

A STUDENT CASEBOOK TO ISSUES, SOURCES, AND HISTORICAL DOCUMENTS

Lynn Domina

The Greenwood Press
"Literature in Context" Series
Claudia Durst Johnson, Series Editor

GREENWOOD PRESS
Westport, Connecticut • London

Library of Congress Cataloging-in-Publication Data

Domina, Lynn.
  Understanding A raisin in the sun : a student casebook to issues,
sources, and historical documents / Lynn Domina.
      p. cm.—(The Greenwood Press "Literature in context"
  series, ISSN 1074–598X)
    Includes bibliographical references and index.
    ISBN 0–313–30349–5 (alk. paper)
    1. Hansberry, Lorraine, 1930–1965. Raisin in the sun.
  2. Domestic drama, American—History and criticism. 3. Afro-
  American families in literature. 4. Afro-Americans in literature.
  I. Title. II. Series.
  PS3515.A515R335   1998
  812'.54—dc21   98–13975

British Library Cataloguing in Publication Data is available.

Library of Congress Catalog Card Number: 98–13975
ISBN: 0–313–30349–5
ISSN: 1074–598X

First published in 1998

Greenwood Press, 88 Post Road West, Westport, CT 06881
An imprint of Greenwood Publishing Group, Inc.

Printed in the United States of America

The paper used in this book complies with the
Permanent Paper Standard issued by the National
Information Standards Organization (Z39.48–1984).

P

Copyright Acknowledgments

The author and publisher gratefully acknowledge permission for use of the following material:

Excerpts from "Abraham Lincoln: Unfinished Business" in *America*, February 8, 1964, pp. 183–84. Reprinted with permission.

Excerpts from "Patterns of Employment Discrimination" by Herbert Hill in *The Crisis*, March 1962, pp. 136–47. Reprinted with permission. The author wishes to thank The Crisis Publishing Co., Inc., the magazine of the National Association for the Advancement of Colored People, for authorizing the use of this work.

"Desegregation in the North" in *The Commonweal*, July 5, 1957, p. 342. Reprinted with permission.

"Detroit Legalizes Discrimination" in *The Christian Century*, September 23, 1964, p. 1164. Copyright © 1964 Christian Century Foundation. Reprinted by permission from the September 23, 1964, issue of the *Christian Century*.

Excerpts from "I Sell My House: One Man's Experience with Suburban Segregation," by Alan Wood. Reprinted from *Commentary*, November 1958, pp. 383–89, by permission; all rights reserved.

Excerpts from "Gentlemen's Agreement in Bronxville" by Harry Gersh. Reprinted from *Commentary*, February 1959, pp. 109–16, by permission; all rights reserved.

Excerpts from "The Significance of African Freedom for the Negro American" by Phaon Goldman in *The Negro History Bulletin*, October 1960, pp. 2, 6. Property of The Associated Publishers Inc. Reprinted with permission.

Excerpts from "Africa in the Thought of Negro Americans" by Dr. Earl E. Thorpe in *The Negro History Bulletin*, October 1959, pp. 5–10, 22. Property of The Associated Publishers Inc. Reprinted with permission.

Excerpts from *The Africans* by David Lamb. Random House. Copyright © 1982 by David Lamb. Reprinted by permission of Brandt & Brandt Literary Agents, Inc.

Excerpts from "Excavating Our History: The Importance of Biographies of Women of Color" by Margaret B. Wilkerson in *The Black American Literature Forum*, Spring 1990, pp. 73–84. Reprinted by permission.

Excerpts from "The Day the 'Race War' Struck Chicago" by Nathan Hare in *The Negro History Bulletin*, March 1962, pp. 123–25. Property of The Associated Publishers Inc. Reprinted with permission.

Excerpts from "Images of Men in Lorraine Hansberry's Writing" by Steven R. Carter in *The Black American Literature Forum*, Winter 1985, pp. 160–62. Reprinted by permission.

"Quit Worrying" by Matthew Cooper in *The New Republic*, October 23, 1995, p. 12. Reprinted with permission.

Contents

Introduction

Intro KP 1

When *A Raisin in the Sun* opened on Broadway in 1959, it became the first play by a black woman ever to be produced in a Broadway theater. Running for a total of 530 performances, the play also won the New York Drama Critics Circle Award. It was adapted as a film in 1961 and presented as an American Playhouse television production in 1989. It has since become a frequently assigned text in high school and college literature courses, and it continues to be performed in a variety of venues throughout the country.

Although it was written *before* the height of the civil rights movement during the 1960s rather than in response to it, *A Raisin in the Sun* raises several critical issues with which the United States and the world would grapple over the coming decades. Indeed, a person could open nearly any contemporary newspaper or news magazine and see these same issues debated despite the different contexts. The most prominent issue raised in the play is integration versus segregation, particularly in regard to housing. When the play was initially performed most areas of the United States were segregated in fact, and many were segregated by law. Although the law has changed during the intervening years, the degree to which the fact of segregation has changed is at best debatable; no one could reasonably argue that the United States has achieved a color-blind society in any arena.

A subplot of the play concerns the relationships among Africans and African Americans. In 1959, African nations were beginning to agitate for independence from their colonial occupiers. Although every African state would achieve its independence within a remarkably short time once the process had begun, most of those same nations have since suffered consistent or intermittent political and economic instability, in addition to other less-measurable effects of colonialism. Simultaneously, however, African Americans have begun to celebrate African cultures much more prominently, as evidenced by events as diverse as the teaching of Afro-centrist philosophy in universities, the sale of clothing with African patterns in department stores, and the recognition of the Kwanzaa holiday within mainstream culture. Inevitably, as the place of Africa within the culture of African Americans has shifted, it has also shifted within the minds of other Americans.

Yet another cultural issue raised presciently by Hansberry in the play involves the roles of men and women, an issue that would also explode during the decade following the play's initial production. In the play the ability of each character to achieve his or her primary goal is connected not only to race but also to gender. Since each of these issues remains so volatile in contemporary American culture, it is no wonder that the play remains so current.

Yet *A Raisin in the Sun* is not simply about issues; it is not simply a sermon disguised as dialogue. Most significant, the play concerns the lives of several fully developed characters. Hansberry created each member of the Younger family with weaknesses and strengths that evoke an audience's sympathy. Men who have felt frustrated with their career options will understand Walter; women who have felt frustrated by a cultural dismissal of their personal aspirations will understand Beneatha; anyone who has agonized over a family's unity will understand Mama. By virtue of the realism and depth of these characters, this play will engage audiences long after the tension surrounding discrimination in America has been resolved.

This study begins with a literary analysis of the play, attending especially to the structure of the play and its themes. Chapters 2 and 3 both consider its historical context. Chapter 2 analyzes the history of segregation and integration in the United States, addressing segregation in employment and education as well as in housing. Chapter 3 explores the relationships among Africans and

African Americans. It contains articles that address the issue philosophically as well as articles from well-known individuals, such as W.E.B. Du Bois and Marcus Garvey, affiliated in one respect or another with the back-to-Africa movement.

Chapter 4 situates the play within the context of the literary tradition of Chicago. As the city has been a major geographic hub for the country, it has also provoked a wealth of literary response, much of which challenges the city to reform. Chapter 5 explores the issue of gender in African American relationships and includes several documents that are comparatively contemporary. Subsumed within this discussion is the question of how African American men and women define their place within families. Finally, Chapter 6 examines contemporary race relations, focusing on topics that have arisen in the play. These include the possibility of minority-owned businesses, the role of alcohol and other addictive substances in African American communities, and the effects of discrimination within the educational system. Each chapter concludes with a list of suggested projects for written or oral exploration, many of which are interdisciplinary in nature, and a list of resources for further reading.

NOTE

Page numbers in parentheses refer to the Signet edition of Lorraine Hansberry's *A Raisin in the Sun*, published in 1988.

Does *RIS* accurately depict postwar ~~housing~~ ~~&~~ struggles ~~for~~ for racial integration, particularly in housing?

1

Literary Analysis

DREAMS DEFERRED

The epigraph of this play consists of several lines from one of Langston Hughes's most famous poems, "Montage of a Dream Deferred." (An epigraph is a generally brief quotation a writer sometimes includes at the beginning of a piece of literature as a comment on the theme or concerns of the work.) The play's title, *A Raisin in the Sun*, is also taken from this epigraph. In his poem Hughes questions whether people simply surrender to circumstances when their aspirations are frustrated or whether those dreams retain their power and erupt in unpredictable ways only after frustrations accumulate. Although many writers choose to use epigraphs, not all of them are as thematically significant to the work as the one Hansberry has chosen. Some writers, for example, use as an epigraph a phrase or line that was influential in their creation of the work but that does not seem to comment directly on it. Hansberry's epigraph, however, asks a question that the play attempts to answer—and the answers vary from character to character. Especially after Walter Younger, the most significant male character in the play, loses the insurance money, some characters seem dangerously close to losing hope, whereas others seem to smolder, waiting for a spark to ignite their barely repressed anger.

Each of the major characters (and some of the minor ones) has a dream, and these dreams urge the plot forward. Mama's dream to own a home with a yard big enough for a garden is one that she has nurtured for years—and that has been deferred for years. She remembers moving into the apartment (where the play takes place) with her husband when they believed the residence would be only temporary. Yet she lived her entire married life there, and it is only through her husband's death that her dream has a chance of being realized (because of the life insurance payment). And Mama remembers the death of their son Claude as the occasion that nearly caused her husband's dreams to die, as if, realizing that he himself would likely not achieve all his desires, he had invested his hopes for a better future in his son. Later in the play, after the insurance money has been lost, Mama tries to make the best of the situation. She tries to persuade herself that the family's situation isn't really so bad—despite the shared bathroom, the living room that also serves as a bedroom, the rats that haunt the alley. Mama says, "this place be looking fine" (140). As if to demonstrate that her own dream has finally died, she continues, "Sometimes you just got to know when to give up some things" (140).

At times her son Walter too seems to have given up, but his surrender fails to quench his anger sufficiently. He dreams of being an independent man, of being his own boss, at least of rising above the servant class wherein his only option is to say "yes, Sir." Although he probably recognizes that his desire to be like the white men who make lucrative deals over lunch in expensive restaurants is unrealizable, his conversation with his own son, Travis, after Mama agrees to give Walter some of the insurance money reveals his desire to attain the respect of class. The Youngers, he predicts, will not only own a Chrysler that is "elegant" rather than "flashy," but they'll employ a gardener (109). And by the time Travis reaches college age, Walter will be ready to "hand you the world!" (109).

Mama chooses to give Walter some of the family's money in part because she witnesses how his failed dreams have begun to crush him. Rather than let go of them, he internalizes his dreams until they consume his spirit. His frustration reveals itself as he begins to shout rather than converse, and he subsequently enacts a stereotypical African as a result of his drunkenness. That is, he resorts to exaggerated dialect, crawls around on his knees, and refers to white men as his masters. Later in this scene, when George Murchison, a boyfriend of Walter's sister, Beneatha, describes Walter as "wacked up with bitterness," Walter responds that he is a "volcano" (85); in other words, his individual power is about to become destructive. Crucially, however, Walter begins leaving the house every morning without going to work. Instead, he drives south to Gary, Indiana; he drives north to Wisconsin; he walks around his own neighborhood newly conscious of the situations of his neighbors; and he ends up each day at a bar. Most shocking to Mama, however, is Walter's lack of response to his wife Ruth's threat to have an abortion; it was bad enough that Mama's husband was nearly destroyed by the death of his child, but worse, Walter has given up hope not only for himself but for his progeny. He has begun to believe that his efforts have no point. He will be able to assume responsibility for his family again only to the extent that he can believe his life presents real choices.

Several years younger than Walter and without substantial responsibility for anyone but herself, Beneatha still believes the world offers her a variety of choices. As she reveals to Joseph Asagai, an African friend with whom she develops a romantic relationship, she once witnessed a friend severely injured in a sledding accident, and his return from the hospital formed the genesis of her dream to become a doctor. Although almost every decision made by every other character during the course of the play is influenced by race, and some are additionally influenced by gender, Beneatha seems not to consider the unlikelihood of a black woman's being admitted to a medical school at this point in history. Although the family sometimes treats this dream as just another whim like playing the guitar, its early origin indicates that her desire is stronger than a whim. Perhaps she will eventually become disillusioned after she experiences more racism or begins to note a lack of progress toward her dream; perhaps, on the other hand, she will eventually serve not only as a physical healer but also as a psychic one as her family and culture plunge into the 1960s.

Toward the end of the play Asagai offers Beneatha yet another option—to return with him to Africa. In a sense, Beneatha has at her fingertips what Walter has promised Travis—the world. Whether she will achieve any of these dreams is, of course, unanswerable. Yet Beneatha is the one major character in the play who has not yet had to defer her dreams, so hope most freely abides in her.

Part of the difference in the ways these characters respond to frustration may simply be a result of temperament. Mama and Ruth, for example, are apparently more able to accept life as it comes than is Walter. However, another explanation is that frustration accumulates not only over lifetimes but also across generations. Mama retains her hope for as long as she does because she converts hope for her own better life into hope for her children's better lives. Walter sees his life as little different from his father's, and as he looks down a long road into the future he envisions few changes. The dreams of his ancestors become weights on his own shoulders, too heavy to bear. He erupts, having smoldered not for years but for generations.

DRAMATIC STRUCTURE

A Raisin in the Sun is structured according to a conventional scheme during which tension builds until the climax. Generally, fiction and drama that follow this format begin with an exposition that introduces the major characters and themes, continue through a complication during which readers speculate about the eventual outcome, reach a climax that is the point of greatest emotional interest, and conclude with a denouement in which loose ends are wrapped up. Most plays are divided into acts, or contain blocks of action, and each act may be further divided into scenes. When plays are produced on stage, changes in acts are conventionally signaled with the lowering of a curtain. Over the next several pages we'll examine the structure of *A Raisin in the Sun*, paying most attention to how the order of events affects the particular emotional responses of the audience.

Although many of us read plays more often than we see them performed, we should nevertheless keep in mind some significant distinctions between drama and fiction. For a fiction writer, a significant choice is point of view: Should the story be told from an omniscient (or all-knowing) point of view, or by one person, whose view is limited? Whose thoughts should be revealed, and how often? Should the narrator be a character in the story or a presence outside the story? For a playwright, these are moot questions because no character's thoughts are revealed directly, and there is seldom an actual narrator (with the occasional exception of a play in which a character steps out to comment on the action, similar to a voice-over in a film).

Because plays are written almost exclusively in dialogue, we might be tempted to believe that a playwright's only method of character development is through that character's speech. And we can learn many things from a character's speech by virtue of his or her dialect, accent, vocabulary, grammar, and so on. But like fiction writers, playwrights have other strategies available to them; despite the physical limitations of a stage, characters are often shown in action and are often talked about by other characters. Sometimes characters can be described directly through the stage directions, as Hansberry describes Ruth before any character speaks: "disappointment has already begun to hang in her face" (24). Yet most of what we learn in a play is conveyed through dialogue, and for this reason conversations often provide information on multiple levels.

Act One, Scene One

During the opening moments of *A Raisin in the Sun* we are introduced to the members of the Younger family. Even though other characters (e.g., Joseph Asagai, George Murchison, Karl Lindner, or Mrs. Johnson) may appear later in the play and may facilitate significant events in the play, in general the play concerns the predicament of the Younger family. In the first scene each of the Youngers appears and speaks. The major concerns of the plot are also revealed almost immediately. By the end of the first scene the audience has a general idea about the central concerns of the play.

Initially, the opening scene seems to reveal a typically chaotic morning in a family where too many people have to be up and out in too short a time. But within a few lines of dialogue, Walter asks about the forthcoming life insurance check and also refers to a newspaper story about a bomb. At this moment the audience fails to understand the significance of either comment—indeed, the eventual revelation of that meaning is one purpose of the play—but already Hansberry has begun to set up the major conflict. For it is the relationship of these two questions—how to invest the life insurance money for the greatest good of the entire family, and how to live in a city and country where bombs are set

off in the homes of African Americans who move into white neighborhoods—that forms the heart of this play.

In general, conflicts in literature are often classified as occurring
between one character and another, between a character and society, between a character and nature, or within a character him-
or herself. In longer works such as novels and plays, more than
one conflict occurs, although they are likely to be related to each
other. The opening scene in *A Raisin in the Sun* already gives clues
to the major conflict—that between the Younger family and the
society they live in. As readers or audience members, we don't yet
realize the significance of those remarks; this major conflict does
not begin to intensify until the appearance of Karl Lindner, a white
homeowner who lives in the neighborhood where the Youngers
will buy their house, later in the play. We are, however, exposed
to other conflicts within the Younger family that will have an impact on the family's response during the climax.

Hansberry has been careful in the opening scene to have the
characters interact in such a way that their conflicts with each other
are immediately revealed. Ruth criticizes Walter for entertaining his
friends the night before in the living room that serves as Travis's
bedroom, a comment that serves the purpose of revealing the
crowded conditions of the apartment as well as Ruth's disapproval
of Walter's friends. From this scene we understand that the primary hopes of Walter and Ruth may be at odds. Ruth seems practical and responsible, denying Travis an extra fifty cents for school,
whereas Walter tries to respond more playfully, complimenting
Ruth's appearance and giving Travis the money even though he
then has to ask Ruth sheepishly for his own carfare. Yet Walter is
not a stereotypical uncommunicative male; he does attempt to ver-
balize his frustration and his dreams, but rather than comprehend
his longing Ruth hears only the words she has heard repeatedly.
To her, the conversation peaked long ago, and repeating the words
signifies stagnation rather than progress. At this point, however,
Ruth may have access to information that Walter lacks—the fact of
her pregnancy, which may make her even more aware of the family's precarious financial situation.

Before Walter leaves the house, he also has an unpleasant encounter with Beneatha. Their bickering is characteristic of a type
of sibling rivalry that is usually resolved before adulthood, although the fact that as young adults Beneatha and Walter continue

to live at home and remain financially interdependent probably influences their relationship—they interact with each other as children because they remain positioned to some extent as children in this household. But their conversation reveals more than their rivalry. Walter feels unjustly treated because Mama has apparently designated some money for Beneatha's education even though, despite his own hard work and financial contributions to the family, the family disregards or dismisses his dream of owning a business.

After Walter leaves, however, Ruth speaks on his behalf to Mama, indicating that she has not ignored Walter. Ruth recognizes that a part of Walter's spirit will die unless he can believe in a true possibility for change in his life. Mama hesitates, not because she doesn't trust or desire to support Walter but because she objects specifically to the type of business Walter hopes to buy, a liquor store. Within this conversation Mama shyly admits her hope to buy a house that will be large enough for everyone—a dream she had shared with her husband, whose death may now ironically provide the means to realize it (through the life insurance payment).

Before the scene concludes, however, Beneatha introduces another theme—the role of women in the world and the question of the proper relation between men and women. Suggesting that she would never marry the wealthy George Murchison, she shocks Ruth and Mama not only because she contemplates declining an offer of wealth but also because she considers declining marriage in general. Although the audience at this point doesn't know how these themes will be developed or how these conflicts will be resolved, this opening scene with its deceptively simple context of a family's typical morning does effectively introduce the major issues of the play.

Act One, Scene Two

Scene one ends as Ruth faints over her ironing. This piques the audience's interest and introduces an issue that will be addressed in scene two. As scene two opens Ruth has gone to the doctor's, though no one other than Mama is aware of this. When she returns she confirms that she is pregnant, to the dismay of just about everyone except Mama. As if to emphasize the family's impending doom, Beneatha looks out the window and spots Travis chasing a rat in the street. Mama realizes how close the other members of the family are to despair when Ruth reveals that the "doctor" she has seen is not a conventional physician but a woman who has the capability of performing an abortion, an illegal procedure at the time that could subject Ruth to severe criminal penalties. Even worse, Walter doesn't object. Mama calls him "a disgrace to your father's memory," a highly ironic accusation because the material effect of Walter's father's memory—the insurance check that has at last arrived during this scene—facilitates the action of the play (75).

Contained between the ends of this conversation is another significant occurrence, the entrance of the African student Joseph Asagai and his critique of Beneatha. He has brought her a traditional African robe, but his compliments to her are undercut by his description of her hair as "mutilated" (61). Earlier, Beneatha had instructed Mama to avoid comments about Asagai's African background that would seem either ignorant or stereotypical, thereby suggesting that African Americans might be no more knowledgeable about Africa than would white Americans. Asagai's comment places the issue of assimilation as a central issue of the play, even as he merely humors Beneatha's desire to be his intellectual companion as well as, perhaps, his romantic partner.

By the end of Act One, every character has either appeared on stage or been referred to within the conversation of others—every character, that is, except Karl Lindner, who is not yet known to the Youngers. In Act Two the issues raised in Act One will be complicated as the family members make choices in their attempts to resolve their conflicts. During Act Two much of the family's hope for a better life, which has begun to seem possible by the end of Act One, will be converted into utter hopelessness.

Act Two, Scene One

The first scene in Act Two can be divided into two main segments. First, George Murchison arrives to pick up Beneatha for their date. Unbeknown to anyone else Beneatha has cut her hair, which appalls her family and prompts George to make several disparaging remarks about Africa. Meanwhile, perhaps longing for success through association, Walter makes an (admittedly drunken) effort to connect with George, who dismisses his overtures. Offended, Walter responds with hostility, describing George as wearing "faggoty-looking white shoes" (83). Although Beneatha is somewhat distressed at her family's reaction to her new hairstyle, nothing in the scene indicates that she will be permanently wounded by their remarks because she dismisses them as hopelessly out of date while she looks to Asagai for political and cultural guidance.

However, Walter is spinning visibly out of control. Responding sarcastically to Walter's statement that he is a volcano, George refers to him as Prometheus, the Greek god who brought fire to humanity and whose punishment for that act consisted of having birds eat out his liver through eternity. In a sense this reference is apt, for Walter is being internally consumed by forces beyond him. Ruth reaches out to him, but just as they begin to reconcile Mama returns, having made a down payment on a house in Clybourne Park, a white neighborhood.

This fact startles even Ruth, who also had placed her hope in a new home and had urged Walter to be happy for the family. At this point the tension increases dramatically, for the audience begins to understand that this is not simply a struggle among the members of a particular family, each of whom is insisting on his or her own way. The conflict now assumes much broader implications, and the audience begins to suspect that by the end of this play an entire culture will be indicted.

Act Two, Scene Two

In the following scene Mrs. Johnson, a neighbor who lives in the same building, enters and clarifies the Youngers' perspective by representing its opposite. She immediately mentions another bombing that is described in the newspaper (the audience will recall the earlier bombing that Walter had read about). Hardly a supportive friend, Mrs. Johnson speculates that next week's headline will refer to a bombing in Clybourne Park. Within this conversation she refers approvingly to Booker T. Washington, who had argued late in the nineteenth century that African Americans (many of whom would likely have been born into slavery) should develop the skills necessary for manual labor rather than aspiring to professions that required more academic training. Whether Washington's choices were appropriate for the nineteenth century or not, Mama feels that they are not appropriate for the mid-twentieth century. She calls Washington a "fool," applying the term by implication to Mrs. Johnson as well (103). Mama has begun to realize that regardless of how much she insists that Walter has a good job in being a chauffeur, he has nevertheless been forced to function as a white man's servant. Satisfaction in this would be as short-sighted and foolish as Washington's view that all African Americans should be farm hands.

After Mrs. Johnson leaves, Ruth and Mama realize that Walter hasn't been to work for several days. Apologizing to Walter, Mama suggests that she has unintentionally colluded with those who believe African Americans should be nothing but servants. Transferring ultimate authority for the family to him, Mama gives Walter the insurance check and, with it, her blessing on his desire to purchase a liquor store.

Act Two, Scene Three

At this point we are approximately two-thirds of the way through the play, and we are tempted to anticipate a quick and happy ending. Before Act Two concludes, however, tension increases significantly. In scene three Karl Lindner, a white man appointed to speak for the neighbors who live near the house Mama has bought, appears to attempt (politely, of course) to persuade the Youngers not to integrate Clybourne Park; and after he leaves, Walter's friend Bobo enters with the news that their mutual friend, Willy, has apparently absconded with all of the insurance money. Walter, Bobo, and Willy had pooled their money, and Bobo and Willy had agreed to travel to Springfield to apply for a liquor license, but as Bobo reveals, Willy did not meet him as planned. Again, the Youngers are forced into conflict with the preferences and practices of mainstream society and simultaneously into conflict with those whom they know more intimately and trust more personally.

In the play the character of Lindner symbolizes the mass of people who are uncomfortable with their own prejudice and therefore deny it. He could satirically be called a "good" bigot. That is, he doesn't overtly advocate throwing bombs or committing other types of violence, but he nevertheless does have a distinct idea about whom he will call his neighbor. He will be reasonable as long as other people accept his reasoning. When the Youngers refuse his logic and his offer to reimburse them if they will relinquish the new house, Lindner essentially warns them that they've had their chance for a peaceful solution. In doing so, he implicitly threatens them with a more violent response when they move. Because the Youngers at this point insist on their dignity as full human beings rather than accept discriminatory treatment, the play seems to continue heading toward a hopeful conclusion, and the audience begins to anticipate triumph with the Youngers.

Before this triumph can occur, however, the Youngers will be given yet another temptation to despair. By the end of this scene, the money is gone. It would seem that a hopeful ending could occur only through an implausible event, but so far the play has stuck close by realism.

Act Three

Act Three consists of only one extended scene during which the climax occurs and several minor conflicts are also resolved. Asagai attempts to raise Beneatha's sights, not simply by asking her to accompany him to Nigeria but also by suggesting that some causes are worth dying for. Although the Youngers' situation isn't as dramatic as Asagai's—they are attempting only to buy a house rather than to revolutionize a nation—they will likely be risking their lives if they move to Clybourne Park. Moreover, one could argue that attempts at integration during the 1960s, historic events mirrored by the literary events in this play, did in fact have revolutionary effects in the United States.

Walter has invited Karl Lindner to return, and he intends to accept Lindner's offer to repurchase the house from the Youngers against the will of the rest of his family. Nevertheless, he vehemently insists that he is a man, echoing the assertions of his slave ancestors. Here the play again implies that although a century has passed since the Civil War, little has changed; the question remains the same: Is a dark-skinned person as human as a light-skinned person? Beneatha, on the other hand, refers to Walter as a "toothless rat," echoing the earlier scene during which Travis chased a rat through the street (144). Walter has psychologically become his society's prey.

When Lindner arrives, however, and Mama insists that Travis witness the surrender of his father, Walter rediscovers his dignity. Even though their impending move may be financially as well as psychologically challenging, the Youngers choose to accept the risks that dignity (i.e., refusing to acquiesce to an inferior social status) demands. The climax has been achieved. The moving trucks arrive. Two pages before the end of the text, or approximately two minutes before the end of the performance, the audience feels a sense of denouement. Whether or not Beneatha goes to medical school or Africa or both, whether or not Walter ever owns a liquor store or any other business, the Youngers will purchase their own home and will integrate a white neighborhood.

Some critics interpret this as a particularly positive and hopeful, almost rosy, ending. Others believe that although the Youngers have chosen wisely and have triumphed morally, they nevertheless will continue to suffer. Their neighbors-to-be, through Lindner's visit, have already indicated that the Youngers are unwelcome. Perhaps they will be subjected to violence. Nevertheless the play does conclude positively, in that the Youngers have chosen justice and dignity over fear.

TOPICS FOR WRITTEN OR ORAL EXPLORATION

1. This entire play occurs in the Youngers' apartment. Write a paper analyzing the effect of this setting on the play.

2. Imagine you are the stage manager for a production of this play. Make a list of all the props you would need. Create a floor plan for the apartment, and describe how you would arrange the furniture, considering especially what you might change between acts in order to enhance the mood.

3. Write a description of the street on which the Youngers live. How many other buildings are on their block? What kind of buildings are they? What kinds of automobiles drive down this street? What is present in addition to buildings (e.g., signs, fire hydrants, streetlights, trash baskets, trees, bushes, sidewalks, etc.)? Be as specific as possible.

4. Imagine you are the casting director for a Broadway or Hollywood production of this play. What actors would you hope to assign to each role? Why?

5. Choose the scene in this play in which you believe each major character most clearly reveals his or her true nature. Analyze the dialogue in that scene, and explain how the scene is most characteristic.

6. Create some scenes that are currently missing from the play. Examples might be the neighborhood meeting attended by Karl Lindner, a date between Beneatha and George or Asagai, the morning Bobo is waiting for Willy at the train station, or the day Mama moved into this apartment with her husband.

7. Create the "background story" of one or more of the characters. That is, what crucial events have occurred in this character's life before the play opens?

8. Assume the point of view of one of the characters in the play, and describe another character. For example, how would Travis describe his mother or father? How would George Murchison describe Ruth or Mama?

9. Make a list of references in the play that are unfamiliar to you. Look up those people, places, or events in an encyclopedia or other source. In a group, discuss how this information enhances your understanding of the play.

10. Drama is a highly structured genre. In order to become more conscious of this structure, watch several television shows or movies, paying attention to how scenes and acts are divided. Compare various

types of shows—sitcoms, tear-jerkers, crime thrillers—according to how the plots are structured. Consider how tension is created and where the climax occurs.

11. Do a similar analysis comparing two or three other plays you have read. How do five-act plays, for example, differ from three- or one-act plays?

12. Read other modern plays and compare their uses of setting with that of *A Raisin in the Sun*. Some plays you might consider include *Death of a Salesman* by Arthur Miller, *A Streetcar Named Desire* by Tennessee Williams, and *Trifles* by Susan Glaspell.

13. Plays depend almost entirely on dialogue to achieve their effects. Choose a work of fiction—a short story or a novel—and attempt to convert it into a play. Aim to keep your stage directions as minimal as possible.

14. Examine the scenes in this play in which clothing and style are discussed. Write an essay examining how you reveal aspects of your own identity through your clothing.

15. Read several poems by Langston Hughes, and compare the thematic issues raised to those Hansberry quotes in her epigraph.

16. Write a story, essay, poem, or play that answers the question: What happens to a dream deferred?

17. Write a brief biography of one of your relatives or of someone else you know well who has had to relinquish a particular dream. What effect has that decision or circumstance had on this person?

SUGGESTED READINGS

Abramson, Doris E. *Negro Playwrights in the American Theatre, 1925–1959*. New York: Columbia University Press, 1969.

Ashley, Leonard R.N. "Lorraine Hansberry and the Great Black Way." In *Modern American Drama: The Female Canon*, ed. June Schlueter. Rutherford, NJ: Fairleigh Dickinson University Press, 1990, 151–60.

Barthelemy, Anthony. "Mother, Sister, Wife: A Dramatic Perspective." *Southern Review* 21, no. 3 (Summer 1985): 770–89.

Carter, Steven R. *Hansberry's Drama: Commitment amid Complexity*. Urbana: University of Illinois Press, 1991.

Cheney, Ann. *Lorraine Hansberry*. Boston: Twayne, 1984.

Keyssar, Helene. *The Curtain and the Veil: Strategies in Black Drama*. New York: Burt Franklin, 1982.

———. "Rites and Responsibilities: The Drama of Black American

Women." In *Feminine Focus: The New Women Playwrights*, ed. Enoch Brater. Oxford: Oxford University Press, 1989, 226–40.

McKelly, James. "Hymns of Sedition: Portraits of the Artist in Contemporary African-American Drama." *American Quarterly* 48, no. 1 (Spring 1992): 87–107.

Nemiroff, Robert. "From These Roots: Lorraine Hansberry and the South." *Southern Exposure* 12 (September/October 1984): 32–36.

Phillips, Elizabeth C. *The Works of Lorraine Hansberry: A Critical Commentary*. New York: Monarch Press, Simon and Schuster, 1973.

Shinn, Thelma J. "Living the Answer: The Emergence of African American Feminist Drama." *Studies in the Humanities* 17, no. 2 (December 1990): 149–59.

Washington, J. Charles. "*A Raisin in the Sun* Revisited." *Black American Literature Forum* 22, no. 1 (Spring 1988): 109–24.

Wilkerson, Margaret B. "Diverse Angles of Vision: Two Black Women Playwrights." In *Intersecting Boundaries: The Theatre of Adrienne Kennedy*, eds. Paul K. Bryant-Jackson and Lois More Overbeck. Minneapolis: University of Minnesota Press, 1992, 58–75.

———. "The Sighted Eyes and Feeling Heart of Lorraine Hansberry." *Black American Literature Forum* 17, no. 1 (Spring 1983): 8–13.

Willis, Susan. *Specifying: Black Women Writing the American Experience*. Madison: University of Wisconsin Press, 1987.

2

Historical Context: Integration and Segregation in the United States

CHRONOLOGY

1861–65	Civil War years.
1866	Ku Klux Klan established in Tennessee.
1870	Passage of Fifteenth Amendment to U.S. Constitution prohibiting racial discrimination in voting.
1882	Chinese Exclusionary Act banning Chinese immigration to the United States for ten years.
1896	*Plessy v. Ferguson* Supreme Court decision permitting "separate but equal" public racial facilities.
1907	Supreme Court declares that railroads have the right to segregate passengers.
1909	National Association for the Advancement of Colored People (NAACP) founded.
1911	National Urban League founded.
1919	Race riots in Chicago.
1924	Immigration Act establishing quotas based on national origin.
1927	Urban League organizes boycott of stores refusing to hire blacks.
1943	Race riots in Detroit.

1946	Supreme Court declares that segregation on buses is unconstitutional.
1947	Jackie Robinson becomes first African American to play major league baseball.
1948	President Truman issues executive order integrating armed forces.
1949	Supreme Court rules that local "covenants" enforcing segregated neighborhoods are unconstitutional. National Housing Act addressing substandard housing.
1954	*Brown v. Board of Education* Supreme Court ruling that "separate but equal" doctrine regarding school segregation is unconstitutional.
1955	Bus boycott in Montgomery, Alabama.
1957	School desegregation crisis in Little Rock, Arkansas.
1960	"Sit-ins" begin at Woolworth's in Greensboro, North Carolina.
1961	"Freedom Riders" attempt to force integration in Alabama.
1962	African American student James Meredith is denied admission to the University of Mississippi, resulting in contempt charges against the governor of Mississippi.
1963	George Wallace's "school house stand" attempting to block integration of the University of Alabama.
	Martin Luther King Jr. arrested in Birmingham, Alabama, while leading civil rights demonstrations.
	March on Washington, D.C., demonstrating for civil rights.
	Medgar Evers assassinated.
1964	Twenty-Fourth Amendment to the Constitution ratified, abolishing the poll tax.
	Martin Luther King Jr. wins the Nobel Peace Prize.
	Race riots in Harlem.
1965	Malcolm X assassinated.
	Martin Luther King Jr. leads march from Selma to Montgomery, Alabama.
	Race riots in Watts, Los Angeles.
	Immigration law abolishes quota system.
	Voting Rights Bill passed.

1967	Black Power conference held in Newark, New Jersey.
	Race riots in Cleveland, Newark, and Detroit.
1968	Civil Rights Act of 1968 guaranteeing fair treatment in housing.
	Martin Luther King Jr. assassinated.

Although many people associate the struggle for civil rights by African Americans most strongly with the decade of the 1960s, the issues that were engaged during that era had long been debated in the United States. Nevertheless, significant changes in civil rights legislation and practice did occur during the late 1950s and 1960s. The frequency with which African American citizens were forced to negotiate major and minor acts of discrimination began to be addressed in the mass media and by important public figures. Thus, it is not surprising that the first play by a black woman to reach Broadway had its plot organized around and found one of its themes in fair housing.

A RAISIN IN THE SUN AND INTEGRATION $Del, Rept.^{\#}$

Although the problems the Youngers face because of segregation seem prominent in the play (and for many readers remain the most memorable aspect of the play), in terms of lines or scenes the actual attention given to integration and segregation is comparatively minimal. Indeed, Mama says that she "just tried to find the nicest place for the least amount of money for my family" (93). And near the end of the play Walter Younger states that "We don't want to make no trouble for nobody or fight no causes" (148). Although the Youngers' act (i.e., deciding to move to an all-white neighborhood) may have had political effects, their motive was not primarily political. It is to Karl Lindner, the sole white character in the play, that race itself constitutes the crucial factor determining where the Youngers should and should not live.

From the beginning of Act One, the consciousness of the Youngers centers more on poverty and wealth than it does on race (although race and class are clearly connected in this play and in the United States). In the stage directions to scene one, Hansberry indicates that the Youngers' apartment lacks many physical comforts—the carpet is worn, the kitchen and living room are only nominally separated, the rooms are lit by a single window. There are not enough bedrooms for the three generations who share the apartment, and they must all share the hall bathroom with other families in the building. Yet the furnishings have been cared for; in fact, part of their wear comes from having been cleaned so much. The audience understands that these characters have attempted to establish a pleasant home despite nearly insurmountable obstacles.

Within a few lines of dialogue, Walter asks about the insurance check. At this point the audience doesn't understand the significance of the check—that it is the life insurance payment due after the death of Walter's and Beneatha's father and Mama's husband, and that it will be for a substantial amount of money. Soon, though, the check is revealed to be a focal point of the characters' obsessions. For each member of the family the check signifies possibility, though their individual hopes differ and at times conflict. The issues of race and, implicitly, segregation enter the play as the characters elaborate on their desires, for their possibilities are not unlimited. The business investment Walter wants to make is one of the few that are open to him as a black man in Chicago. Although Beneatha is a college student, many colleges were segregated in 1959, and even those that admitted African American students often adhered to a quota system. Further, Mama's decision to purchase a house in an all-white neighborhood raises the issue of segregation explicitly. In a sense, then, the issue of integration enters the play because of the economic characteristics of segregation rather than as an example of abstract moral justice. If Mama had been able to purchase a comparable house for a comparable price in a black neighborhood, she might not have considered moving to the all-white neighborhood of Clybourne Park.

Many comments demonstrating the characters' frustration early in the play illustrate the effects of segregation before that topic is addressed directly. In Act One, scene one, Walter reveals his discouragement: "I got a boy who sleeps in the living room— . . . and all I got to give him is stories about how rich white people live" (34). Class parallels race, Walter implies, so even if he were to become wealthy, he'd never live in the luxury of "rich white people." Other characters also rely on the phrase "rich white," indicating that to them "rich" cannot be separated from "white." Urging Mama to buy herself a trip to Europe or South America,

Ruth says, "rich white women do it all the time" (44). But Mama's response is, "Something always told me I wasn't no rich white woman" (44). As the play will demonstrate, *how* white people live is closely related to *where* they are able to live.

When Mama broaches the possibility of purchasing a house, she suggests that she could get a job herself. She probably means domestic service, cleaning the house of another (presumably white) woman. Ruth also works as a domestic. Walter works as a chauffeur, which he describes as dull and monotonous and depressing. His description reveals that his job suppresses any sense of individuality or desire for initiative, that it positions him as utterly powerless. Although Mama has attempted to encourage Walter at this moment by suggesting that he has a good job, she acknowledges the validity of his perspective during her subsequent conversation with Mrs. Johnson. Although she may remain uncomfortable with the prospect of Walter investing in a liquor store, she remembers that her husband would have agreed with him. Mama acknowledges that even the "good" jobs that are open to African Americans are degrading. The status of "rich white" people depends in part on their ability to employ men and women like Walter and Mama as their servants. These conversations reveal the systemically pervasive nature of segregation; to be effective, it must function in many arenas—schools and employment, for example, as well as housing.

Karl Lindner's role illustrates not only the insidious nature of segregation but also the various strategies employed by segregationists. He does not want to be viewed as a bomb-throwing, crossburning racist; rather, he perceives himself as logical, courteous, and just—after all, he is willing to reimburse the Youngers for their investment by purchasing the house from them. He asserts that people should talk with one another, learn to understand one another. Rather than commit violence, he hopes the Youngers will understand his perspective—although he doesn't concern himself with understanding theirs. And although he supports segregation, he doesn't want to be categorized as a racist, for he claims that "race prejudice simply doesn't enter into it. . . . [O]ur Negro families are happier when they live in their *own* communities" (118). Unwittingly he has reversed his vocabulary, for he represents white families who believe they will be happier if they can live "in their own communities." In other words, Lindner is uncomfortable with overt racism but even more uncomfortable with integration when it applies to his own neighborhood.

After Walter loses the family's money, the question of whether they will integrate Clybourne Park (by becoming its first black residents) seems to become moot. Walter arranges a meeting with Lindner in order to accept his offer; the family will then at least recover some of their $10,000. By the time Lindner arrives, however, Walter has had time to reflect on his family's history, on his father's determined pride, and on the contributions his ancestors have made to America. Rather than articulate his new understanding with political slogans, he attempts to tell his family's story to Lindner, whose only response is a veiled warning.

Although some readers interpret the conclusion to *A Raisin in the Sun* as unequivocally positive, there is reason to believe that the Youngers' life in their new home will be tense, even dangerous. They are clearly unwelcome, and they have been warned to stay away. Given the context of contemporaneous U.S. historical events, they may have to tolerate racial slurs, vandalism to their property, even personal violence. Nevertheless, this conclusion to the play is more optimistic than if Walter, Mama, and the others had remained in a state of psychological surrender. As the play ends, Walter especially has assumed agency; that is, he has realized that in the face of injustice—even injustice supported by much of his culture—he is capable of fighting back.

— *Perspective #1*

INTEGRATION AND SEGREGATION IN THE UNITED STATES

Civil rights bills had been passed during the first half of the twentieth century, as well as during the nineteenth century, and several cases addressing discrimination had reached the Supreme Court. In one form or another, the issues raised in these cases had been debated openly and whispered about privately since the United States first began to identify itself as an independent nation. Part of the tension developed because of a cultural inability to agree on the meaning of "equality." Even staunch abolitionists during the early to mid-nineteenth century disagreed on the extent of social integration that should follow emancipation. By today's standards, Abraham Lincoln, despite his statements in the Emancipation Proclamation and the Gettysburg Address, would not be considered radical—at a celebration of his second inaugural, for example, black people were prohibited from entering until a white senator intervened to procure an invitation for Frederick Douglass, an ex-slave who had run away and become an outspoken proponent of abolition. During and following the Civil War, three amendments to the Constitution were passed that sought to establish greater equality between black and white citizens. The Thirteenth Amendment, passed in 1861, outlaws slavery; the Fourteenth Amendment, passed in 1868, declares that all people born or naturalized in the United States are citizens—and therefore claim the rights of citizens. In 1870 the Fifteenth Amendment was passed; it states that the right to vote cannot be withheld from a person on the basis of race. These amendments, however, were circumvented in the years following Reconstruction by numerous Jim Crow laws in the South that mandated separate public facilities for members of different racial groups, as well as by other forms of institutionalized racial discrimination throughout the country.

Individuals who urged America to work toward increased integration disagreed over strategy. While some racial leaders urged black citizens to be patient, to adapt to the philosophy of gradualism (an idea that will be discussed further in the next chapter), others demanded more immediate change, arguing that they had already been waiting for centuries. Nevertheless, by the time Lorraine Hansberry was writing *A Raisin in the Sun* in the 1950s, racial segregation was pervasive throughout the United States. Although her play primarily addresses discrimination in housing, this form of segregation cannot be divorced from segregation in its other forms—in employment, in schools, in public transportation, and so on. And the fact that she set her play in Chicago (in part for autobiographical reasons) illustrates the fact that race was not simply a southern issue, as many northerners preferred to believe. Nor was housing segregation limited to distinctions between black and white citizens; some neighborhoods also excluded a wide range of ethnic and religious groups, including Italians, Asians, and Jews.

Segregation in housing, however, had broad effects. A child's address often determined where he or she would attend school; segregated neighborhoods meant segregated schools even if integration was not legally proscibed. And even today, where a person lives often affects where he or she can be employed; if the majority of high-paying jobs are in white, suburban neighborhoods with little access to public transportation, black, inner-city residents are forced into more local, lower-paying jobs. Even if a black person did become wealthy, however, he or she generally had access only to poor housing. This was especially true in the North, for in the South black neighborhoods traditionally included a broader range of housing. Ironically, ghetto prices were (and remain) high because the areas were so confined. More people than could be accommodated needed housing in black neighborhoods; thus, demand exceeded supply. And even today, because much housing in inner cities is available for rental rather than purchase, landlords (who generally do not live in the neighborhood) have little incentive to maintain their property.

Despite many attempts at civil rights legislation, the Supreme Court case with the most profound influence on segregation was *Plessy v. Ferguson* in 1896. In this decision the Court declared that "separate but equal" public facilities were constitutional. Whether or not separate facilities could be equal in theory, in practice they never were; but this philosophy held until the 1954 case of *Brown v. Board of Education*, in which the Court ruled that separate school systems were "inherently" unequal. In 1924 the National Association of Real Estate Boards decided that it would be unethical for its members to facilitate the sale of homes in white neighborhoods to members of minority groups, making the assumption that such a sale would result in declining property values (an assumption that was often faulty). This had the effect of maintaining segregated neighborhoods even when property owners were themselves willing to sell to African Americans or other minorities. Subsequently "restrictive covenants" became popular, in which communities agreed to limit sales of houses to members of specific racial and ethnic groups. These local covenants were enforced by state and national courts until the Supreme Court ruled them unconstitutional in 1948. However, a national preference for integration could not be effective unless a policy of nondiscrimination was enforceable under national law, in addition to state or local laws. Title VIII of the 1968 Civil Rights Act specifically covers fair housing.

Although national laws are often most effective because the federal government can require compliance with nondiscrimination policies as a condition of access to government contracts, laws such as the Civil Rights Act of 1968 would never have been passed without the work of numerous local civil rights groups. Fair housing organizations existed in many cities and municipalities during the 1960s. Their members often included religious leaders as well as prominent businesspeople—and these organizations were effective in part because of the credibility of their individual members. As in many other situations, people were willing to take a controversial stand once others had already done so.

Even though it is no longer legal anywhere in the country to refuse to sell or rent property to a person on the basis of his or her race or ethnicity, many areas of the United States remain segregated in practice. Cities such as New York, Chicago, and Los Angeles contain neighborhoods that are almost exclusively white or exclusively black. Some states, especially those in the Great Plains or northern New England, have particularly low minority populations. And the social lives of many people continue to be segregated; even when they live and work in integrated situations, they socialize primarily or exclusively with members of their own race. Nevertheless, some of the changes that have occurred on both the national and local levels might have seemed inconceivable when Hansberry wrote *A Raisin in the Sun*.

The Arguments

Research into the history of racial discrimination reveals a striking similarity between the arguments of integrationists and segregationists. Both groups, for example, found justification for their views in the Bible and religious tradition. Both groups asserted a rationale of individual rights to reach their opposing conclusions—segregationists arguing that an individual should be able to sell a home as he or she sees fit, and integrationists arguing that an individual should be able to buy any home he or she can afford.

Arguments in support of segregation shared many assumptions with racist thought in general. Supporters of segregation drew their ideas from a variety of sources, including science, history, psychology, literature, and religion. Many of these arguments were most prominent during the late nineteenth and early twentieth centuries, and their supporters had the goal not only of enforcing social segregation but also of depriving black citizens of the right to vote and otherwise participate in the political life of the nation. These arguments remained current in mainstream media even after scientists had discounted the so-called scientific evidence, which included analysis of body type in relation to intelligence and evolutionary states. Although much of the segregationists' reasoning was circular (e.g., white is good because it's white; or "kinky" hair is inferior to straight hair because straight hair is affiliated with white skin, and white skin is intrinsically superior), their inevitable goal was to demonstrate that black people were so innately inferior to white people that social integration and political equality would inevitably be detrimental to the nation.

Characteristics associated with white people were invariably used as a standard, and racists evaluated every difference from that standard as inferior. After demonstrating that members of various races looked different, these racists (unsuccessfully) sought to prove that the internal organs, particularly the brains, of white and black people also differed. Although scientists soon abandoned this project, others did seek to certify the intellectual inferiority of African Americans through the use of intelligence testing, a practice that emerged during the early twentieth century. IQ (intelligence quotient) tests remain controversial, and many people argue that their questions are biased toward white and male test-takers.

Although the ideas espoused by scientists, psychologists, and historians were often published in scholarly journals with limited circulation, they reached a mainstream audience through the cooperation of novelists and other writers. Novelists such as Thomas Dixon provided a voice for segregationists in such books as *The Leopard's Spots* (1902) and *The Clansmen* (1905). Because readers often view novels exclusively as entertainment, they are less likely to question the assumptions and arguments present in the text—and hence are more likely to accept them. In writing *A Raisin in the Sun*, therefore, Lorraine Hansberry was participating in a long tradition of addressing American race issues through literature.

Segregationists feared that if integration occurred, miscegenation—marriage between a black person and a white person—would soon follow, as the character Ruth acknowledges when she suggests that the new neighbors are afraid of intermarriage. Although it had been frequently acknowledged that white slave masters had sexual relations with their black slaves, segregationists asserted that black men experienced an uncontrollable desire for white women. If black men were permitted to associate with white women on an equal basis, they contended, marriages and children would inevitably occur—and the eventual result would be the weakening of the white race. In other words, African influence would dilute the natural superiority of white Americans.

Although segregationists could cite very little scientific or historic evidence for this argument, they could rely on the support of many ministers and theologians, possibly the most influential group of professionals to support segregation. Just as some Americans had relied on the Bible to justify slavery, their descendants used the Bible to justify segregation. Racists stated that segregation was the will of God, and they generally argued either that God had created entirely distinct races from the beginning or that the Book of Genesis, properly interpreted, insisted that God had ordained that various races be separated soon after the creation of Adam. By arguing that segregation was the will of God, they implied that all moral Christians should support it. More liberal churches, at least until the 1960s, often avoided discussing such a troubling issue.

In terms of white homeowners, the most powerful argument against integration was that as soon as a black family moved into a neighborhood, property values would begin to fall. Because of this fear, many middle-class white Americans supported segregation regardless of their feelings about integration on a moral or political level. They worried that they would fail to recoup their investment if they should decide to sell their homes. In addition, because property taxes are based on the value of a house or land, if property values fall so do tax revenues. Anything supported by tax revenues, such as schools, would subsequently suffer financial strains. Stereotypes regarding black people (e.g., that they would neglect property they did purchase, creating a neighborhood eyesore) often fed this fear.

People who supported integration attempted to address this anxiety. When property values fell after a black family moved into the neighborhood, they pointed out, the change was not precipitated by the mere presence of black people but rather by "white panic." That is, so many white property owners reacted by putting their homes up for sale simultaneously that supply far exceeded demand, and prices dropped. When white property owners refused to participate in panicked selling, property values remained stable throughout the integration process. This argument made sense to people who were calm enough to recognize logical appeals, but in the highly charged context of racial integration, emotional responses often prevailed.

Like segregationists, integrationists also looked to the Bible for support. Rather than cite specific verses, they more often interpreted the Bible holistically. They understood the Bible to say that all people are created equally by God and that all people should be treated respectfully and lovingly. Although Martin Luther King Jr. in his "Letter from Birmingham Jail" reprimanded white mainstream ministers for failing to take a more visible stand in support of integration, the white leadership that did emerge in support of civil rights often came from religious institutions and organizations. Although some ministers feared that contributions to their collection plates would decrease if they openly supported integration, others discovered that financial support of their churches actually increased when they began to openly address racial justice. These priests and ministers often wore their clerical collars when they participated in protest marches, readily identifying themselves as moral leaders in order to appeal to the conscience of observers.

Other protesters looked to the Declaration of Independence, the United States Constitution, and the Bill of Rights and based legal actions on those documents. Although many laws permitting segregation had been passed by state legislatures and upheld by courts, integrationists continued to argue that such laws were unconstitutional. Even if such laws were legally permissible, integrationists declared, they were contrary in spirit to American values. If Americans truly believed in their national rhetoric—that "all men are created equal," that America is a land of "liberty and justice for all"—then they must abandon the hypocrisy of segregation. Eventually this view prevailed in the landmark civil rights legislation that was passed during the 1960s.

The following documents explore the arguments and circumstances surrounding segregation during the 1950s and 1960s. First are two articles that contextualize the civil rights movement within U.S. history and culture. They are followed by an excerpt from *The Southern Case for School Segregation*, which attempts to present the tradition of segregation as reasonable. The next group of documents consists of editorials protesting legislation that permits housing segregation. Next is an excerpt from Toni Morrison's novel *The Bluest Eye*, which presents the response of an African

American woman working as a domestic for a white family. Following this, two articles examine the effects of housing discrimination on Jewish families. Finally, excerpts are included from national legislation passed during this era that addresses housing discrimination.

PERSPECTIVES ON CIVIL RIGHTS AND SEGREGATION

The next three excerpts present a range of opinion regarding integration during the early 1960s. Throughout the country at this time, many people agreed philosophically that integration was an issue of justice but nevertheless hesitated to support any practical steps in the direction of integration. Many other people, of course, refused to believe that integration would be good for the country and argued instead that segregation was a morally acceptable choice. Although many writers spoke specifically about housing discrimination or educational discrimination or employment discrimination, most Americans understood these issues as being related.

EDITORIAL FROM *AMERICA*

In this editorial, the editors of *America* magazine argue that African American citizens remain enslaved, in a sense, because they do not yet enjoy the full privileges of citizenship. Although the editors may be attributing more progressive attitudes to Abraham Lincoln than he in fact held, they refer to Lincoln in order to appeal to his status as a national hero and in order to remind readers of the generations that have passed since the Civil War without seeing any substantial progress in terms of civil rights.

They argue that the time has arrived for change, that "reasonably soon" must be immediately, that "gradualism" has already taken so long that it in itself is unjust. They also refer to a practice that has come to be known as affirmative action. Because white citizens and institutions have so deprived African Americans of equal opportunities, the editors assert, African Americans must currently be compensated with additional opportunities in order to level the playing field.

FROM "ABRAHAM LINCOLN: UNFINISHED BUSINESS"
(*America*, February 8, 1964)

The work of Lincoln will finally be done only when the American Negro is at last fully freed from the bondage of slavery. Emancipation was formally decreed on January 1, 1863, and three million slaves were given a new life by the adoption, December 18, 1865, of the Thirteenth Amendment. A century has rolled by since then, but we are not yet through with the long process of translating these high principles into palpable elements of genuine equality and opportunity for the nearly 20 million American Negroes of 1964.

• • •

In order to help our Negro brothers pull themselves up out of the subnormal status to which they have been condemned by the segregation the rest of us devised, we now have to *exaggerate* efforts at intensive remedial education, job-training and the building of confidence and morale. And let no one think that this can be done without heroic effort on the part of Negroes and an almost complete about-face in the attitudes of most of their white fellow citizens.

Talk is cheap. But actually getting this job done reasonably soon is going to be immensely expensive in time, money, energy, imagination and purposeful hard work. We say "reasonably *soon*" because, while a project of this kind cannot be accomplished overnight, we have wasted so much precious time already that comfortable old slogans of a discredited "gradualism" have no more meaning. The work must be done now. (183)

HERBERT HILL'S ANALYSIS

In this article, which was originally published in *The Crisis*, a magazine published by the NAACP, Herbert Hill analyzes the effects of discrimination in employment. Regardless of how responsible or talented a Negro worker is, by virtue of the color of his skin he remains unqualified for many higher-skilled and hence higher-paying jobs. Even if he is hired for a better job, housing discrimination colludes with employment discrimination to guarantee that he can only work on less prestigious projects since only white workers were permitted in white neighborhoods. Because so many corporations operate in several states, Hill suggests that the only solution is a national law outlawing these practices.

FROM HERBERT HILL, "PATTERNS OF EMPLOYMENT
DISCRIMINATION"
(*The Crisis*, 1962)

As a result of . . . discriminatory provisions, white persons are usually hired initially into production and skilled craft occupations which are completely closed to qualified Negro workers. The Negro worker who is hired as a laborer in the "maintenance department" or "yard labor department" is denied seniority and promotional rights into production classifications and is also denied admission into apprentice and other training programs. In these situations Negro seniority rights are operative only within certain all-Negro departments and Negro workers therefore have an extremely limited job mobility. Thus, a Negro worker with 20 years seniority in a southern steel mill, papermaking factory, tobacco manufacturing plant or oil refinery, may be "promoted" only from "toilet attendant" to "sweeper." . . . (139)

Quite frequently, Negroes are excluded altogether from work in white neighborhoods. This means that Negro carpenters for example are restricted to marginal maintenance and repair work within the Negro community and that they seldom are permitted to work on the larger industrial and residential construction projects. . . . (143)

It is our considered opinion that the dual objectives of significantly reducing employment discrimination and simultaneously improving manpower utilization throughout the American economy can be achieved more rapidly and effectively under an all-embracing national fair employment practices law than under a variety of state and municipal laws. A basic characteristic of American private enterprise is that it is organized predominantly on a national rather than on a state or local basis. . . . (145)

In the North as well as in the South there is a direct relationship between poverty and discrimination and the federal government must intervene to eliminate both of these related evils which endanger American society. (147)

JAMES JACKSON KILPATRICK'S ARGUMENT

A resident of Virginia, a powerful Southern state that has historically wielded significant conservative influence in the area of race relations, James Jackson Kilpatrick has written a book that summarizes much thought during the 1950s and early 1960s regarding racial difference. He draws on science, anthropology, and psychology as well as history and law. With the goal of explaining southern thought to northerners, whom he perceives to be uniformly liberal, he presents an argument regarding states' rights that is similar to the one the Confederacy presented during the Civil War. While claiming to accept the school desegregation order of *Brown v. Board of Education* issued in 1954, Kilpatrick simultaneously urges the country to make changes slowly rather than suddenly through legislation.

In the passage below, he implies that African Americans have suffered through their own fault. Relying on stereotypes, he asserts that African Americans are simply incapable of success and that national decisions should be based on how things are rather than on how they ought to be. Although a concept like equality may be attractive in theory, he suggests, such an idea simply won't work on a practical level.

FROM JAMES JACKSON KILPATRICK, *THE SOUTHERN CASE FOR SCHOOL SEGREGATION*
(The Crowell-Collier Press, 1962)

The reality that the South has had to cope with most constantly . . . is the reality of the Southern Negro. Other races of men, caught at the bottom of the ladder, have clambered up. The identical decades that saw Negroes set free in the South saw the Irish set down in New England. "No Irish need apply." The signs hung outside New England mills as uncompromisingly as the "white only" signs outside an Alabama men's room. Who would have imagined in, say, 1880, that a Boston Irish Catholic would be President? But the Irish fought their own way up, on merit and ambition and hard work. They *made* a place at the table. They won acceptance, and they paid their own way.

No such reality has been visible in the South. Instead of ambition . . . we have witnessed indolence; instead of skill, ineptitude; instead of talent, an inability to learn. It is very well for social theorists to say of Southern Negroes that they are *capable* of this, and their *potential* is for that, and if it were not for segregation and second-class citizenship and denial of opportunity, they would have achieved thus and so; but the Southerner . . . is not so much interested in determining a point of metaphysics. . . . [H]e has to be concerned with reality.

The first reality he faces squarely is the one reality most often shunned: the *inequality* of man. . . . The South holds small enthusiasm for egalitarian doctrines based upon the infinite perfectibility of man. . . . Theoretically, to be sure, men are born to equal rights; but empirically, for good or ill, these rights are incapable of equal exercise. . . . These are realities, and the Southerner as Realist accepts them. (35–36)

OPPOSITION TO SEGREGATION IN HOUSING

As integration in housing became a prominent issue during the 1950s and 1960s, newspapers and magazines throughout the country regularly printed editorials addressing the subject. Traditionally, editorials are unsigned and are understood to represent a consensus opinion of the publication's editorial staff. Because of space limitations, these editorials tended to be succinct and to address aspects of the issue that were considered most important to the readers. Each editorial reprinted below briefly summarizes a local situation, after which the editors directly and adamantly oppose moves to reinforce segregation.

EDITORIAL FROM *THE COMMONWEAL*

This article contains several ideas that are representative of popular thought regarding segregation during the late 1950s: that real estate agents agitate against integration, that the South and the North remain enmeshed in a battle over race, that individual rights serve as the foundation for the discussion. In this editorial the writer refutes the commonly held notion that integration negatively affects property values. The writer then acknowledges that homeowners do have rights but argues that those rights are not absolute. However, a significant portion of the editorial is devoted to retaining distinctions between the North and the South—because once the North and South become perceived as equally unjust, northerners will lose their credibility on the issue of race. Needless to say, this is a debate between white northerners and white southerners; in this as in many contemporaneous mainstream publications, African Americans do not speak but rather are spoken for.

"DESEGREGATION IN THE NORTH"
(*The Commonweal*, 1957)

New York City has for many years led the nation in the fight against racial discrimination, and it is now attempting to take still another step in banning segregation from the city's housing. A bill was introduced in the City Council which would make racial discrimination illegal even in privately owned apartment houses. As a result of protest, however, chiefly from the city's Real Estate Board, the bill has been withdrawn for revision.

We are sorry that the New York City Council has been swayed by the real estate men. Their first argument against the bill is the old, long-discredited claim that desegregation will depress property values. Experience has shown that such a result comes about only when interested parties permit it to, and prevention of slum areas conserves and stabilizes property values. The second argument is that the bill is an invasion of privacy, and infringes the right of a private citizen to rent his property to anyone he chooses. This objection is slightly more valid, but obviously no citizen may exercise a right to the clear detriment of the rights of others, and this is the case here. Further, in New York a privately owned restaurant, for instance, has the legal right to impose reasonable restrictions on the patrons it will serve but may not discriminate on the basis of race. And an apartment house seems no more privately owned than a restaurant.

What is unfortunate about the New York controversy is that publicity concerning it has furnished aid and comfort to white supremacists in the South. Southern segregationists are fond of calling attention to the beam in the Northern eye in the matter of racial inequalities, and they can now cite the position of the New York Real Estate Board as paralleling their own.

This is not the case. No one in New York is denying the constitutionally guaranteed right of a citizen to free use of unquestionably public facilities and utilities, and this right is being denied in the South. We disagree with the opponents of the New York bill, but even as we do we must point out in fairness that their position is not that of the White Citizens Councils. The New York bill, which we hope will soon be passed, represents a trail-blazing extension of already far-reaching civic responsibility for minority rights. (342)

EDITORIAL FROM *THE CHRISTIAN CENTURY*

This editorial refers to a Detroit "homeowners rights ordinance," which was similar to "restrictive covenants" that were common in other cities, including Chicago. Although in *A Raisin in the Sun* the character Karl Lindner represents a neighborhood alliance that expects voluntary compliance in housing segregation rather than legal sanctions, these covenants were essentially also agreements among white homeowners not to sell property to African Americans. Although such laws may not have existed when segregation could be taken for granted, some homeowners and real estate agents instigated such legislation precisely when integration began to seem likely. Ironically, while some "gradualist" racists urged America to wait for integration until it occurred "naturally" rather than force it through legislation, these homeowners sought to prohibit it through legislation just when it did seem to be occurring naturally.

By mentioning Catholic, Protestant, and Jewish organizations that opposed the ordinance, the editorial seeks to persuade readers of the full moral authority of its stance. Additionally, by referring to the agreement of Michigan's governor and Detroit's mayor, the writer implies that the ordinance suffers from broad-based opposition and that despite the fact that voters passed it, only those on the fringe of society could be expected to support such an idea.

"DETROIT LEGALIZES DISCRIMINATION"
(*The Christian Century*, 1964)

By a vote of 137,671 to 114,743 Detroit voters recently adopted a "homeowners rights ordinance" which in effect legalizes racial discrimination in housing. The ordinance had been condemned as immoral by the Roman Catholic bishops of Michigan, the Metropolitan Detroit council of churches and the Metropolitan Detroit Jewish community council. The crucial phrase in the ordinance guarantees to the property owner "the right to maintain what in his opinion are congenial surroundings for [himself], his family and his tenants" and "the right to freedom of choice of persons with whom he will negotiate or contract with reference to such property, and to accept or reject any prospective buyer or tenant for his own reasons." The constitutionality of this discriminatory ordinance, obviously designed to keep Negroes out of white communities, should be tested immediately and, if necessary, all the way to the United States Supreme Court. The Ordinance flies in the face of federal restrictions against restrictive covenants and subjects the basic rights of minority peoples to the whim of predominant majorities. The new ruling was opposed by Michigan's Governor George Romney and Detroit's Mayor Jerome Cavanagh. In Illinois a similar referendum was eliminated by the state board of elections on the grounds that the petition for the referendum raised two questions and provided for only one answer. In California, Proposition 14, supported by the California Real Estate Association, will, if adopted by the people in the general election, repeal the California fair housing law. The Detroit ordinance and California's Proposition 14 are based on the assumption that the people can treat the elemental right of a minority as they please if they vote to do so. This assumption profanes democracy and violates constitutional restrictions which protect the rights of the individual against the caprices of the multitude. (1164)

THE CHARACTER OF PAULINE IN *THE BLUEST EYE*

The Bluest Eye by Toni Morrison is a novel whose protagonist, Pecola, a young African American girl, is victimized by her position in the culture. Raped by her father and ostracized by her neighbors, she eventually loses her mental stability, a process the novel traces as it examines the factors contributing to Pecola's situation. Pecola's mother, Pauline, like Ruth Younger in *A Raisin in the Sun*, is employed as a domestic in a white family's home. Unlike Ruth, however, Pauline aligns herself with her white employers because the pleasures in their home are so much more significant and because the hope in her own world is so slim. Although she is never fully part of her employer's family, her only avenue to respect is through them.

FROM TONI MORRISON, *THE BLUEST EYE*
(New York: Simon and Schuster, 1970)

[Pauline] became what is known as an ideal servant, for such a role filled practically all of her needs. When she bathed the little Fisher girl, it was in a porcelain tub with silvery taps running infinite quantities of hot, clear water. . . . No zinc tub, no buckets of stove-heated water, no flaky, stiff, grayish towels washed in a kitchen sink, dried in a dusty backyard. . . . Soon she stopped trying to keep her own house. The things she could afford to buy did not last, had no beauty or style, and were absorbed by the dingy storefront. . . . Here she could arrange things, clean things, line things up in neat rows. Here her foot flopped around on deep pile carpets, and there was no uneven sound. Here she found beauty, order, cleanliness, and praise. . . . She reigned over cupboards stacked high with food that would not be eaten for weeks, even months; she was queen of canned vegetables bought by the case, special fondants and ribbon candy curled up in tiny silver dishes. The creditors and service people who humiliated her when she went to them on her own behalf respected her, were even intimidated by her, when she spoke for the Fishers. She refused beef slightly dark or with edges not properly trimmed. The slightly reeking fish that she accepted for her own family she would all but throw in the fish man's face if he sent it to the Fisher house. Power, praise, and luxury were hers in this household. . . . It was her pleasure to stand in her kitchen at the end of a day and survey her handiwork. Knowing there were soap bars by the dozen, bacon by the rasher, and reveling in her shiny pots and pans and polished floors. (100–101)

SEGREGATION AFFECTING JEWS

Although African Americans were the most frequent and obvious victims of discrimination, they were not the only ones. Many "restrictive covenants" also forbade selling homes to Asians, Italians, or Jews. Even in the absence of legal restrictions, many Jews found it difficult to purchase homes in Gentile or Christian neighborhoods. Although Jewish identity isn't as easily recognizable (despite some stereotypes) by Gentiles as African American identity generally is by whites, Jewish family names often were enough to make real estate agents wary.

ALAN WOOD'S NARRATIVE

Alan Wood is the pseudonym for a man who purchased a home in a middle- to upper-middle-class neighborhood on Long Island. At the time, his suburb was populated by both Jewish and Christian residents. Within a few years, however, the area became predominantly Jewish. When Wood decided to sell his home in the 1950s, he faced an ethical quandary—should he inform potential Gentile buyers that the neighborhood was almost exclusively Jewish? His assumption was that non-Jewish people would be unhappy living in the neighborhood. The gradual segregation of Wood's neighborhood had occurred without violence or even the threat of it, almost without notice. Although Wood supports integration, he is disturbed that his experience seems to support the character Karl Lindner's position in *A Raisin in the Sun*—that people do seem to prefer living among others who resemble them.

FROM ALAN WOOD, "I SELL MY HOUSE"
(*Commentary*, 1958)

... I happened to inquire why his original owner had moved. "He was a Gentile," my neighbor said. It seemed to him to constitute full and sufficient explanation.

Some time later I had occasion to meet this Gentile, whose taste in landscaping I had long admired, and I asked him why, if he loved the community as much as he professed, he had left. He was quite frank about it. He was perfectly happy to live in a mixed neighborhood, he said, until one day his wife gave a birthday party for his daughter and asked all the neighbors' children to come. "Of the thirty-two children invited, thirty were Jewish," he said. "Somehow that didn't seem a natural environment in which to raise my children." (384)

• • •

Although the community was hardly homogeneous, in one respect it had assumed its own brand of conformity: whenever a house was sold it was to Jews, and across our street all three Gentile families had moved away. (385)

• • •

Had we sold the house? Mr. Wilson asked anxiously, because if not he wanted to buy it. When we got down to terms, they couldn't have been better. He was offering close to the asking price, he had the cash differential between our figure and the existing mortgage, he wanted to move in as fast as we wanted to move out. Still, it was only Sunday morning and—who knew?—maybe the ad would pull someone who would offer us even more. I asked Mr. Wilson to talk to his bank and call me Monday evening. I hung up the phone and told my wife. She looked at me.

"What are you going to do?" she said.

"What do you mean, *do?*"

"I mean Mr. and Mrs. Wilson are Christians," she said. "Are you going to tell them about the neighborhood?"

I have always considered myself an ethical person. For some reason, perhaps because it so strongly involved religious considerations, I chose to regard this as an ethical question. But ethics were something you rarely discussed abstractly at study groups, temple breakfasts, or Great Books (my one "interfaith" activity, since it was the only place I could meet local Christians). How could ethics resolve my peculiar dilemma?

What made it worse was that, by now, I badly wanted to sell the house. Far from being sure it would be only a question of accepting the highest bidder, I foresaw not only a lot of lost weekends but the very real possibility of a last-minute squeeze which would shave thousands off my price. I had a bid in hand, but was afraid that if I described the community the Wilsons would fly away. So for the first time since my wife and I had visited him before moving to NSCH [North Shore Community Homes], I phoned the rabbi for a professional visit. He was out of town.

My wife in the meanwhile was going through the NSC [North Shore Community] phone book. To our pleasant surprise, quite a few non-Jewish families appeared to be still living in the community. Unfortunately none in our particular area; our section was solidly Jewish. I was beginning to realize the irony of our situation. Discrimination worked in reverse in NSCH. I stood to lose a sale because my customer was a Gentile. (385–86)

· · ·

The pattern was a familiar one. Communities that started out mixed would maintain their proportions for a while; then, almost before anyone realized it, a selling wave would sweep the area and, all at once, it would become populated with members of a single faith. As a matter of fact, the problem had become so acute in our own area that our Ministers Board had instituted a study of ways to arrest this one-sided migration. (387)

· · ·

"Frankly," the minister said, "our worst problem is brokers. They're the ones who give the terrific impetus to making communities one-sided. Once they decide an area is predominantly Jewish or Catholic, they perpetuate the situation by showing houses only to Jews or Catholics. And there's nothing we can do about it." (387)

· · ·

So I could talk about it at last. And because she [Mrs. Wilson] had raised the question, not because she spared me from having to bring it up (that no longer mattered), and since it showed she was aware of the situation, I told her everything I had learned. I told her about the estimated percentage, about the presence and location of other Gentiles, about my talk with the minister, and that I knew he and everyone else would do everything in their power to make the Wilsons feel at home. (389)

· · ·

When I hung up, it was with great shame. After all my pious moralizing, I had succumbed to the same fear I deplored. I had had so little faith in myself and in my neighbors I was convinced that once the Wilsons learned the truth they would never want the house. These people had made me feel humble; by God, I was proud of being a blockbuster, and I had reason to believe some of my neighbors would feel proud, too. Between us and the ministers we'd make sure the Wilsons were wanted in NSCH. There would be a victory—albeit a modest one—for integration on Candytuft Lane.

Which makes the outcome of the Wilson affair all the more anticlimactic; but then fact *is* stranger than fiction, and, with the obvious exception of names and places, everything in this report is true. Early the next morning, my wife got a call from Wilson, who was intensely apologetic. On the way to our place to close the deal, it seems they passed an area they had never investigated. They saw this house for sale and—to make a long story short—they bought it on the spot. It was my neighbor who stressed the fact that it was located in the most restricted Gentile town on Long Island. (389)

HARRY GERSH'S EXPERIENCE

A "gentlemen's agreement" indicates a practice that demands conformity, or cooperation, but that is not written down. It need not be put in writing because "gentlemen" do not betray their word. During the 1950s, Harry Gersh had heard rumors that such an agreement existed in Bronxville, a small town in the suburbs north of New York City, and that this agreement precluded the sale of homes to Jews within the incorporated limits of the town. Because of the configurations of social and economic power in and around New York, anyone who broke this agreement could expect a loss of status and business. In addition, Gersh refers to the "Lawrence complex"; this was a group of businesses including utilities and investment firms. These companies were founded by one man, William V.D. Lawrence, and the family still controlled them. They owned nearly all of the available rental units in Bronxville. In other words, residents of Bronxville did not need to threaten violence against any Jewish people who attempted to move into the neighborhood, because they had already threatened the psychic lives of each other. Gersh's several failed attempts to purchase a home in Bronxville indicated that these rumors were indeed founded in fact. Although many of the people with whom Gersh spoke did not want to be perceived as bigots, they nevertheless cooperated with an agenda of segregation.

FROM HARRY GERSH, "GENTLEMEN'S AGREEMENT IN BRONXVILLE"
(*Commentary* 1959)

. . . Bronxville . . . is unique in one respect. It doesn't like Jews and won't admit them as residents.

There are other areas in Westchester, Nassau, and other suburban counties around New York which try to stay demonstrably "Aryan." But these are places without sharply defined boundaries; their exclusionary practices are being steadily eroded. Bronxville, on the other hand, is an incorporated village, with legal boundaries within which Jews are unwelcome, except as visitors or customers. (109)

• • •

Bronxville's social pattern, as we shall see, includes real estate anti-Semitism: to break it is to betray your friends and neighbors, people who would remain friends even after you left Bronxville. The community includes important figures in most industries; to incur their enmity in Bronxville might later cause you trouble on Park Avenue or Wall Street. Rigid enforcement of the rule against Jews does not require the active assistance of the majority of the population, but it does require—and evidently commands—the majority's assent. Finally, the dominance of the Lawrence complex in the real estate of the village, and possibly in other matters, may be a factor in enforcing the "Gentlemen's Agreement." (111)

• • •

Lower Westchester county accepts Bronxville's anti-Semitism as a fact of life. I have not heard even of any Jewish organizational protest. A few weeks ago, I decided to test the validity of this acceptance. I decided to try to buy a house in Bronxville. (112)

• • •

Some phrases have become so clichéd that you don't expect to hear them from normally aware persons. "Some of my best friends are Jews" is one which I heard several times that day, and this agent was the first to use it.
"Some of my best friends are Jews," she said. "And I wouldn't want you to be hurt. It's not even you and your wife so much. You're probably used to it. But your children. You know how cruel children can be. Think of your son and daughter exposed to the cruelty of the other children." (113)

• • •

Some time later, I asked a non-Bronxville real estate operator what would have happened had I insisted on buying one of the houses that had been shown to me. He assured me that the deal would have fallen through at some point. By the time I could get my wife up to see the house, it would have been sold or taken off the market. If I had insisted on putting down a binder immediately, the agent would have accepted it subject to the owner's approval—which would not have been given.

And, if I had passed these and a few other hurdles, I might have had trouble getting a local mortgage at favorable terms.

One Bronxville resident took issue with the conclusions I drew from my experiences with the real estate agents. They did not speak for all Bronxville, he argued. His argument did not impress me. Real estate operators are in business to make money. One, two, or even three of the five I visited might be so bigoted as to refuse to do business with a Jew. But their unanimity, as well as their *ex parte* comments, showed that more than real estate agents' prejudices were involved. These people were expressing a community feeling, following instructions from community leaders who could enforce them. The Jew who bought a house from a builder, and then had to move, was not made "uncomfortable" by real estate agents. (115)

· · ·

When I offered the socio-psychological thesis on which the Supreme Court based its desegregation order—that segregation, even with equal facilities, is bad for the children of both the segregated and the segregating groups—he said that he had seen no evidence of this among Bronxville's students. Bronxville's graduates, he maintained, were as "liberal" (his word) as their peers from more heterogeneous schools.

Despite this educator's informed view, his statement is open to serious question. Most children growing up in a community which openly says "we do not want Jews as neighbors" come to accept this attitude as right and just. Certainly, some children will question it, as they question all the verities propounded by their parents. But most do not examine too deeply. They accept the gentlemen's agreement and assume that it is one of the things that makes Bronxville living so pleasant—like having money, cars, servants, and straight teeth. There remains the disturbing possibility that if, on leaving Bronxville, they should ever lack money or cars or servants, they may decide to blame their deprivations on having to live among Jews. (115–16)

CIVIL RIGHTS LEGISLATION

Since the Civil War but more particularly during the second half of the twentieth century, the U.S. Congress has passed several pieces of legislation attempting to guarantee all citizens equal access to rights and privileges consistent with American values. Simultaneously, the Supreme Court has struck down numerous pieces of legislation it has deemed discriminatory. The debates surrounding some of these laws would have informed the writing of *A Raisin in the Sun*. The fact that many of these laws include the phrase "race, color, religion, or national origin" indicates that all these categories were frequently grounds for discrimination. Although some of the laws may seem wordy or redundant and may hence be difficult to follow, their apparent redundancy can be seen as an attempt to close loopholes that might otherwise tempt some individuals into breaking the spirit if not the letter of the law.

HOUSING ACT OF 1949

This legislation argues that the good of the nation depends in part on all residents having access to adequate housing. At this point in history (the late 1940s), inadequate housing tended to occur in two categories: slum neighborhoods that were usually populated by minorities, and rural farm housing. The law suggests that integrated neighborhoods would be beneficial to business in general as well as to the housing industry. Later sections of the law provide funding to remedy the problems the law addresses.

FROM "HOUSING ACT OF 1949"
Eighty-First Congress—Sess. 1, Chap. 338, 1949
Declaration of the National Housing Policy

Sec. 2. The Congress hereby declares that the general welfare and security of the Nation and the health and living standards of its people require housing production and related community development sufficient to remedy the serious housing shortage, the elimination of substandard and other inadequate housing through the clearance of slums and blighted areas, and the realization as soon as feasible of the goal of a decent home and a suitable living environment for every American family, thus contributing to the development and redevelopment of communities and to the advancement of the growth, wealth, and security of the Nation. The Congress further declares that such production is necessary to enable the housing industry to make its full contribution toward an economy of maximum employment, production, and purchasing power. The policy to be followed in attaining the national housing objective hereby established shall be: (1) private enterprise shall be encouraged to serve as large a part of the total need as it can; (2) governmental assistance shall be utilized where feasible to enable private enterprise to serve more of the total need; (3) appropriate local public bodies shall be encouraged and assisted to undertake positive programs of encouraging and assisting the development of well-planned, integrated residential neighborhoods, the development and redevelopment of communities, and the production, at lower costs, of housing of sound standards of design, construction, livability, and size for adequate family life; (4) governmental assistance to eliminate substandard and other inadequate housing through the clearance of slums and blighted areas, to facilitate community development and redevelopment, and to provide adequate housing for urban and rural nonfarm families with incomes so low that they are not being decently housed in new or existing housing shall be extended to those localities which estimate their own needs and demonstrate that these needs are not being met through reliance solely upon private enterprise, and without such aid; and (5) governmental assistance for decent, safe, and sanitary farm dwellings and related facilities shall be extended where the farm owner demonstrates that he lacks sufficient resources to provide such housing on his own account and is unable to secure necessary credit for such housing from other sources on terms and conditions which he could reasonably be expected to fulfill.

CIVIL RIGHTS ACT OF 1964

This law addresses several discriminatory practices. The first section addresses voting, especially the issue of literacy tests as a condition of voter registration. Prior to 1964 several states required literacy tests of their constituents who wanted to vote, but these tests were not administered fairly. White citizens and black citizens would often receive different tests, and the tests would be designed to ensure the failure of potential black voters. According to the Civil Rights Act of 1964, if these tests are to be given they must be given *in writing* so that an accurate record of them can be kept.

The law also regulates businesses. Any business open to the public—such as a restaurant, hotel, or theater—is forbidden to discriminate against various population groups. African Americans could no longer be forced to sit in the back of the theater, nor could waiters or waitresses any longer refuse to serve African American customers.

A further section of the law forbids employers to hire on the basis of race. Skin color could no longer legally be considered a qualification for any job.

FROM "CIVIL RIGHTS ACT OF 1964"
(Public Law 88-352, July 2, 1964)

(2) No person acting under color of law shall— ...

(c) employ any literacy test as a qualification for voting in any Federal election unless (i) such test is administered to each individual and is conducted wholly in writing, and (ii) a certified copy of the test and of the answers given by the individual is furnished to him within twenty-five days of the submission of his request made within the period of time during which records and papers are required to be retained and preserved to title III of the Civil Rights Act of 1960. . . . *Provided, however*, That the Attorney General may enter into agreements with appropriate State or local authorities that preparation, conduct, and maintenance of such tests in accordance with the provisions of applicable State or local law, including such special provisions as are necessary in the preparation, conduct, and maintenance of such tests for persons who are blind or otherwise physically handicapped, meet the purposes of this subparagraph and constitute compliance therewith.

• • •

Title II—Injunctive Relief Against Discrimination in Places of Public Accommodation

Sec. 201 (a) All persons shall be entitled to the full and equal enjoyment of the goods, services, facilities, privileges, advantages, and accommodations of any place of public accommodation, as defined in this section, without discrimination or segregation on the ground of race, color, religion, or national origin.

(b) Each of the following establishments which serves the public is a place of public accomodation within the meaning of this title if its operations affect commerce, or if discrimination or segregation by it is supported by State action;

(1) any inn, hotel, motel, or other establishment which provides lodging to transient guests, other than an establishment located within a building which contains not more than five rooms for rent or hire and which is actually occupied by the proprietor of such establishment as his residence;

(2) any restaurant, cafeteria, lunchroom, lunch counter, soda fountain, or other facility principally engaged in selling food for consumption on the premises, including, but not limited to, any such facility located on the premises of any retail establishment; or any gasoline station;

(3) any motion picture house, theater, concert hall, sports arena, stadium or other place of exhibition or entertainment.

• • •

(e) The provisions of this title shall not apply to a private club or other establishment not in fact open to the public, except to the extent that the facilities of such establishment are made available to the customers or patrons of an establishment within the scope of subsection (b).

Sec. 202. All persons shall be entitled to be free, at any establishment or place, from discrimination or segregation of any kind on the ground of race, color, religion, or national origin, if such discrimination or segregation is or purports to be required by any law, statute, ordinance, regulation, rule, or order of a State or any agency or political subdivision thereof.

• • •

Sec. 703. (a) It shall be an unlawful employment practice for an employer—

(1) to fail or refuse to hire or to discharge any individual, or otherwise to discriminate against any individual with respect to his compensation, terms, conditions, or privileges of employment, because of such individual's race, color, religion, sex, or national origin; or

(2) to limit, segregate, or classify his employees in any way which would deprive or tend to deprive any individual of employment opportunities or otherwise adversely affect his status as an employee, because of such individual's race, color, religion, sex, or national origin.

FAIR HOUSING POLICY OF 1968

This amendment to an earlier law addressed several practices that had become common after segregation was legally forbidden. For example, real estate agents sometimes induced white homeowners to sell their homes at a loss by suggesting that the neighborhood was about to become integrated. The real estate agent would subsequently sell the same house at an inflated profit. In other circumstances real estate or rental agents would delay appointments with black individuals, hoping that a white person would appear to buy or rent the property first. Thus, this law is a response to practices that had arisen in attempts to circumvent earlier fair housing laws. The law not only forbids discrimination in housing on the basis of race, but it also specifically addresses some unfair real estate practices, such as lying to members of minority groups about the availability of housing in a given neighborhood.

FROM "TITLE VIII—FAIR HOUSING"
(1968)

Sec. 801. It is the policy of the United States to provide, within constitutional limitations, for fair housing throughout the United States.

• • •

Sec. 804. . . . it shall be unlawful—

(a) To refuse to sell or rent after the making of a bona fide offer, or to refuse to negotiate for the sale or rental of, or otherwise make unavailable or deny, a dwelling to any person because of race, color, religion, or national origin.

(b) To discriminate against any person in the terms, conditions, or privileges of sale or rental of a dwelling, or in the provision of services or facilities in connection therewith, because of race, color, religion, or national origin.

(c) To make, print, or publish, or cause to be made, printed, or published any notice, statement, or advertisement, with respect to the sale or rental of a dwelling that indicates any preference, limitation, or discrimination based on race, color, religion, or national origin, or an intention to make any such preference, limitation, or discrimination.

(d) To represent to any person because of race, color, religion, or national origin that any dwelling is not available for inspection, sale, or rental when such dwelling is in fact so available.

(e) For profit, to induce or attempt to induce any person to sell or rent any dwelling by representations regarding the entry or prospective entry into the neighborhood of a person or persons of a particular race, color, religion, or national origin.

TOPICS FOR WRITTEN OR ORAL EXPLORATION

1. Research the history of your city or neighborhood, focusing on how its ethnic or racial composition has (or has not) shifted. Choose a specific time period to examine, such as the last ten, twenty, or fifty years.

2. The character Lindner states that "a man, right or wrong, has the right to want to have the neighborhood he lives in a certain kind of way" (117). Discuss the differences between "the right to" and "want to." Are there indeed certain rights a person has regarding the nature of his or her neighborhood?

3. Discuss why a person like Lindner would express a desire for segregation while nevertheless claiming that "race prejudice simply doesn't enter into it."

4. Compare the description of the Youngers' apartment at the beginning of the play with descriptions of other houses or apartments in novels, stories, or plays you've read. Some possibilities to consider include *House of Mirth* by Edith Wharton, *Native Son* by Richard Wright, *The Awakening* by Kate Chopin, "A Rose for Emily" by William Faulkner, or *Brown Girl, Brownstones* by Paule Marshall. How do these descriptions contribute to the work's theme?

5. Mama says she "just tried to find the nicest place for the least amount of money for my family" (93). She was not necessarily trying to make a political statement regarding integration. Research the economic and social effects of segregation—effects that go beyond simply separating the races. For example, compare the cost of groceries at an inner city with a suburban grocery store, or look in the classified advertising section of a newspaper to compare the type of housing available for similar prices in different neighborhoods.

6. Write an additional scene that occurs after Hansberry's play ends, a scene that occurs the day after the Youngers move to Clybourne Park.

7. Compare the responses of different religious leaders to the subject of integration. Analyze how people using the same sources, especially the Bible, could reach such different conclusions.

8. Examine newspaper editorials from the 1950s and 1960s. What can you tell about a city based on the issues addressed in these editorials? Compare the representation of events as reported in white and black newspapers (e.g., the Chicago *Tribune* and the Chicago *Defender*).

9. The character Mrs. Johnson compares Chicago to Mississippi. Research the differences in segregation between these two areas or be-

tween two other distinct cities, states, or regions. You may choose
the 1950s when the play is set or a more recent decade.

10. Mama says that "being a servant ain't a fit thing" (103). Write an
essay agreeing or disagreeing with this statement.

11. Define *poverty* and compare your understanding of the condition
with Mama's discussion of the subject. Consider especially Mama's
response to Walter when he wants to buy the liquor store.

12. Interview a real estate agent or fair housing representative about his
or her experience in complying with fair housing legislation. Pay particular attention to the issues that continue to exist despite decades
of fair housing legislation.

13. Write a response to the editorial from *America* or to Herbert Hill or
James Jackson Kilpatrick.

14. Imagine that you are a real estate agent. Write a letter explaining the
actions criticized in "Desegregation in the North."

15. After reading the excerpts from the three laws included in this chapter, select portions that seem redundant and discuss in a group why
these laws might need to be written this way.

SUGGESTED READINGS

Banner-Haley, Charles T. *The Fruits of Integration: Black Middle-Class
Ideology and Culture, 1960–1990*. Jackson: University Press of Mississippi, 1994.

Chappell, David L. *Inside Agitators: White Southerners in the Civil Rights
Movement*. Baltimore: Johns Hopkins University Press, 1994.

Dimond, Paul R. *Beyond Busing: Inside the Challenge to Urban Segregation*. Ann Arbor: University of Michigan Press, 1985.

Franklin, John Hope, and Genna Rae McNeil. *African Americans and the
Living Constitution*. Washington, DC: Smithsonian Institution
Press, 1995.

Griffin, John Howard. *Black Like Me*. Boston: Houghton Mifflin, 1961.

Hecht, James L. *Because It Is Right: Integration in Housing*. Boston: Little, Brown, 1970.

Helper, Rose. *Racial Policies and Practices of Real Estate Brokers*. Minneapolis: University of Minnesota Press, 1969.

Ingram, T. Robert. *Essays on Segregation*. Boston: St. Thomas Press,
1960.

Keppel, Ben. *The Work of Democracy: Ralph Bunche, Kenneth B. Clark,
Lorraine Hansberry, and the Cultural Politics of Race*. Cambridge, MA: Harvard University Press, 1995.

Molotch, Harvey Luskin. *Managed Integration*. Berkeley: University of California Press, 1969.

Moody, Anne. *Coming of Age in Mississippi*. New York: Dell, 1992.

Newby, I.A. *Jim Crow's Defense: Anti-Negro Thought in America, 1900–1930*. Baton Rouge: Louisiana State University Press, 1965.

Sanders, Charles L. "Playing Hooky for Freedom." *Ebony* (April 1964): 153–62.

Steinberg, Stephen. *Turning Back: The Retreat from Racial Justice in American Thought and Policy*. Boston: Beacon, 1995.

Taeuber, Karl E., and Alma F. Taeuber. *Negroes in Cities*. Chicago: Aldine Publishing, 1965.

U.S. Commission on Civil Rights. *Issues in Housing Discrimination*. A Consultation/Hearing of the United States Commission on Civil Rights, Washington, DC, November 12–13, 1985. Volume 1: Papers Presented. Washington, DC: U.S. Government Printing Office, 1985.

von Furstenberg, George M., Bennett Harrison, and Ann R. Horowitz, eds. *Patterns of Racial Discrimination*. Lexington, MA: D.C. Heath, 1974.

Vose, Clement E. *Caucasians Only: The Supreme Court, the NAACP, and the Restrictive Covenant Cases*. Berkeley: University of California Press, 1959.

Wilson, Theodore Brantner. *The Black Codes of the South*. University: University of Alabama Press, 1965.

Woodward, C. Vann. *The Strange Career of Jim Crow*. New York: Oxford University Press, 1957.

3

Historical Context: Africa, Africans, and African Americans

CHRONOLOGY

1441	Portuguese navigators begin slave trade in western Africa.
1455	Cadamosto, navigator from Venice, explores Senegal River.
1470	Portuguese navigators discover Gold Coast, West Africa.
1492	Columbus "discovers" America.
1505	Portuguese open factories on eastern coast of Africa.
1509	Beginning of slave trade in New World.
1618	Founding of Dutch West African Company.
1619	First African slaves in North America arrive in Virginia.
1660	Dutch settle in South Africa.
1712	Slave revolts in New York.
1727	Quakers demand abolition of slavery.
1787	Sierra Leone becomes settlement for free slaves.
1791	Slave revolt in Santo Domingo.
1808	United States ends importation of slaves from Africa.

1820	Liberia founded for African Americans returning to Africa.
1831	Nat Turner leads slave revolt in Virginia.
	William Lloyd Garrison begins publishing *The Liberator*.
1832	New England Anti-Slavery Society founded.
1833	Abolition of slavery in British empire.
1847	Liberia becomes independent republic.
1861–65	U.S. Civil War.
1879	British war with Zulus.
1895	Portions of British South Africa Company become Rhodesia.
1903	England conquers Northern Nigeria.
1960	Nigeria granted independence.
1962	Uganda and Tanganyika attain independence.
1963	Kenya becomes independent.
1964	Zanzibar and Tanganyika unite to form Tanzania.
	Northern Rhodesia becomes independent and is renamed Zambia.
1965	Gambia becomes independent.
1975	Portugal grants independence to its African colonies: Angola, Mozambique, Cape Verde, and São Tomé.

Although the most prominent themes of *A Raisin in the Sun* concern aspects of integration within the United States, a significant secondary issue concerns the relationship between Africans and African Americans. As Hansberry was writing the play, several African countries that were retained as colonies by European nations were beginning to agitate for their freedom. Most of these African countries attained independence during the subsequent decade, although that freedom was often accompanied or followed by violence as political and military leaders struggled for power. In the play the American characters, most notably Mama and Mrs. Johnson, debate the value of the philosophies of some African American heroes. At mid-century, then, Africans were re-evaluating their status as colonial subjects while African Americans were re-evaluating their status as U.S. citizens.

AFRICANS AND AFRICAN AMERICANS IN *A RAISIN IN THE SUN*

The most significant representation of Africa in *A Raisin in the Sun* resides with the character of Joseph Asagai. Before he arrives on stage Beneatha mentions him to Mama, and their conversation debunks any affiliation audience members might assume "naturally" exists between Africans and African Americans. Equally significant, their conversation challenges African Americans to consider their own relationship to Africa. Within this conversation Mama questions why she should be an expert on Africa. (Indeed, in the mid-twentieth century most Americans didn't know any more about Africa than they did, say, about China or New Zealand or Brazil.) To the extent that Mama considers herself primarily an American, she would not be expected to know any more about Africa than any other American would—even though her skin is black.

On the other hand, this scene and subsequent ones imply that knowledge about Africa could empower African Americans. Although as readers or audience members we don't know whether her changes will be permanent, Beneatha alters her way of thinking and acting after meeting Asagai; these shifts anticipate changes that will occur in African American culture during the 1960s. The initial conversation between Beneatha and Mama links the detachment that exists between Africans and African Americans with the effects of colonialism. After initially confusing Nigeria with Liberia, Mama asserts that the money she donates for missionary work in Africa has very little to do with the site as specifically African. She donates money to convert heathens; it's only a coincidence that they're Africans. When Beneatha suggests that the African people could better use protection from colonial powers than they could from heathenism, she is drawing attention to the fact that religious missionaries often functioned in cooperation with European military and governmental authorities as they attempted to dismantle traditional African cultural practices. Beneatha also critiques "popular culture" representations of Africa when she urges Mama to avoid asking Asagai condescending questions that would reveal her attachment to stereotypes. In citing Tarzan as the most common image of Africa, Beneatha reveals the extremity of the problem because Tarzan is a fictional rather than a historic figure. Mama

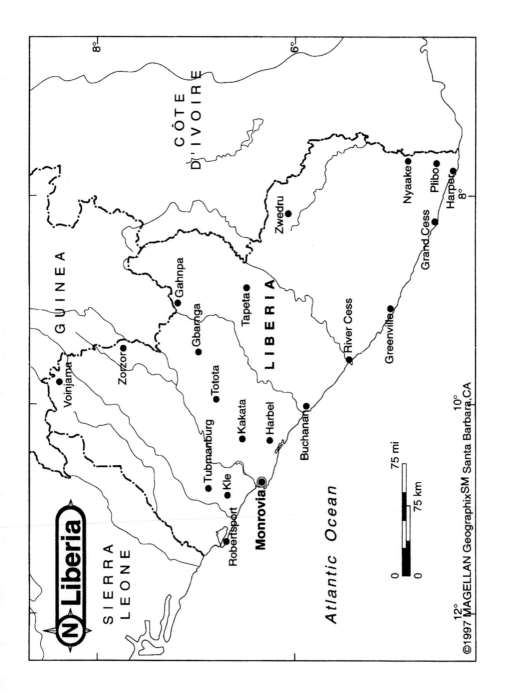

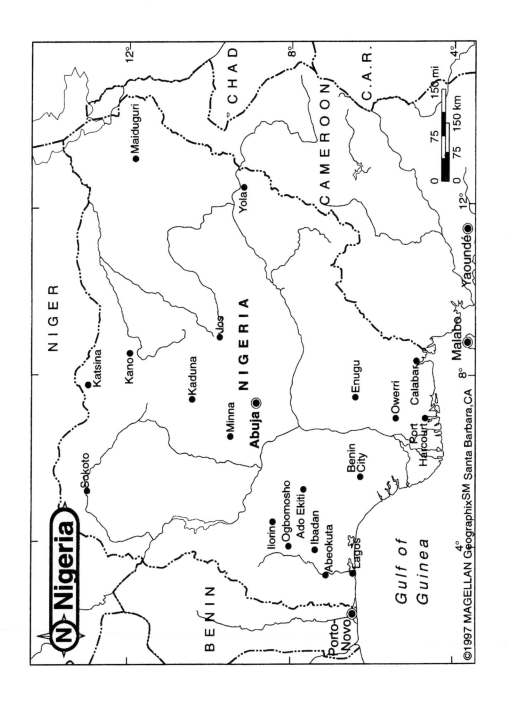

Nigeria

©1997 MAGELLAN GeographixSM Santa Barbara,CA

57

proves herself a quick study, however, for when Asagai arrives she immediately protests, "I think it's so sad the way our American Negroes don't know nothing about Africa 'cept Tarzan" (64).

Thus, the audience is prepared *not* to interpret Joseph Asagai as a mere exotic figure when he appears on-stage. While one could debate the degree to which Beneatha internalizes her new identity as a descendant of Africa as much as she is an American, Asagai is clearly committed to the transformation of Nigeria into an independent nation—although at times his goals also seem self-serving. When a disillusioned Beneatha speaks of giving up, of the impossibility of progress, because it seems that regardless of how hard her family tries, they will never realize their hopes, Asagai shouts, "I LIVE THE ANSWER!" (135). He acknowledges that progress is sometimes difficult to measure or notice. And he acknowledges that violence almost inevitably accompanies significant political change—violence that might result in his own death. But even that, he claims, will be progress.

Asagai has already given Beneatha a Yoruba nickname, and now he gives her an African robe to symbolize the connection between her African descent and her American citizenship. This robe is elegant and intended to enhance her dignity. By the end of the play he invites her to Nigeria to explore her heritage directly; the implication is that should Beneatha visit Africa, she would visit as Asagai's wife. As she considers his offer, she is attracted to both its romantic and its unexpected qualities. However, given her history of fleeting interests (which are explicitly referred to in the play), the likelihood of her actually traveling to Africa is slim.

Just as some Americans imagine Tarzan as Beneatha suggests when they think of Africa, relying on stereotype rather than on direct observation or active study, so some white Americans also interpret the character of African Americans through the lens of stereotype. Ironically, only after Walter Younger descends into the embodiment of this stereotype is he able to cast it off. After he realizes that the insurance money is gone and that the family may be in even worse circumstances than they were as the play opened, Walter imitates—to his family's horror—a groveling plantation Negro: "Captain, Mistuh, Bossman . . . Oh, yassuh boss! Yasssssssuh! . . . Father, just gi' ussen de money . . . —we's ain't gwine come out deh and dirty up yo' white folks neighborhood" (144). However, when Lindner arrives and Mama forces Travis to remain as a witness, Walter's hope for his son's future overpowers his shame at his own present. He does not speak in the dialect white writers ascribe to African Americans, nor does he fall to his knees as an inferior to a superior. He in fact defies the expectations of everyone around him, from Beneatha to Lindner (with the possible exception of Mama, who has continued to believe in him as an individual rather than as a representative of a group).

As the Youngers are attempting to integrate Clybourne Park, even if their reasons aren't political, Asagai critiques the United States by suggesting that African Americans too frequently try to assimilate, or become part of the mainstream. He accuses African Americans of valuing white culture too highly, of attempting to look white and be white rather than celebrating their African heritage. African Americans, he suggests, have internalized the racism that is so prevalent in mainstream American culture. Although the immediate impetus for this comment is Beneatha's straightened hair, he might also critique African American styles of clothing, religious practices, and so on, that imitate those of the majority white culture. The tension in the black community over this issue becomes obvious when George arrives to pick up Beneatha for their date and, shocked at her new haircut, calls her "eccentric" (80). George suggests that "assimilationist" is simply a new term for "Uncle Tom," a reference to a major character in Harriet Beecher Stowe's novel, *Uncle Tom's Cabin*. Although this is an inaccurate description of the character in Stowe's novel, the term has come to mean an African American who betrays others in order to ingratiate himself or herself with whites. George himself reveals his ignorance of African history and culture when he asserts angrily, "your heritage is nothing but a bunch of raggedy-assed spirituals and some grass huts!" (81). This was precisely the attitude that Hansberry and other African American leaders worked to overcome.

Disagreements regarding their African heritage were mirrored in African Americans' disagreements over their American history. When the character Mrs. Johnson hears that the Youngers plan to move, she initially attempts to instill fear in their hearts before revealing her jealousy of their ambition. After Mama suggests that being a servant is undignified, Mrs. Johnson cites Booker T. Washington: "Education has spoiled many a good plow hand—" (103). This remark is disturbingly similar to many slave masters' opinions that education would spoil the slaves; they realized that educated slaves would learn to think critically about their situation and demand their freedom. Similarly, Washington's remark implies that education would encourage African Americans to aspire to higher professional goals, that they would no longer be satisfied with their limited options. Mama has already realized this, and her response is blunt: "The fool" (103). Mama has chosen a more active stance toward her own future than Washington would have advised. She no longer has patience for friends or neighbors who attempt to rein in her drive. Whether or not she ultimately takes an activist stance toward Africa or begins to define herself as an American of specifically African descent, she clearly does begin to demand equal treatment within her society and equal access to its benefits.

AFRICA IN RECENT HISTORY

Africa today consists of approximately forty nations. The cultures of these nations vary widely, in part because of the presence of the Sahara Desert, which has historically made interaction between regions in the north and south difficult. The political structures of these nations vary also, ranging from military dictatorships to democratic republics. Many ancient history classes study the civilization of the Egyptians and look at photographs of the pyramids. Subsequently, though, many history books address African events tangentially, if at all. Africa is mentioned in relation to America during discussions of the slave system and in relation to Europe during discussions of empire and colonialism, but African history itself is seldom taught on its own terms. In discussing contemporary Africa, however, one must address the issue of colonialism, for many African national borders and political structures are a direct result of the European (and, to some extent, American) presence in Africa during the nineteenth and twentieth centuries. Contemporary African boundaries fail to reflect ethnic divisions as many European boundaries do, but rather testify to the competitive agendas of these European countries, especially England and France.

One of the most significant events affecting the current composition of Africa was the Berlin Conference, held in 1884. It was attended by representatives of nearly every European country and the United States, but members of African nations were not invited. The purpose of the conference was to establish trade agreements among European nations; Africa possessed many natural resources that could be exploited by European industry and also had the potential to provide a market for industrialized goods. In other words, Africa was simply the site upon which European countries wrestled each other for increasing power. Although many countries had laid claim to various African regions prior to this conference, and although European countries continued to develop further African colonies subsequent to the conference, some agreements were reached that partitioned the Congo region among Germany, Portugal, France, and Belgium. The conference represents one method through which African borders were established—according to the economic and military convenience of Europeans rather than according to previously existing ethnic or tribal divisions of Africans.

Because Liberia and Nigeria are discussed in *A Raisin in the Sun*, we will spend the next few pages examining those countries. Although no country can be considered representative of Africa in general, the two nations are different enough in their histories and current situations to illustrate the range of African national circumstances. Additionally, although both countries are located in western Africa and border the Atlantic Ocean, their colonial histories are radically different, and a comparison of the two can provide provocative insights.

Liberia

The Independent Republic of Liberia was established in 1847. Aside from Ethiopia, Liberia is the only African country that was never a European colony. However, European traders—including Portuguese, Dutch, German, French, and English—did explore the coast during the fifteenth and sixteenth centuries. In *A Raisin in the Sun*, Mama initially confuses Nigeria with Liberia when she says that Nigeria was the country founded by former slaves. In fact, Liberia is most known for a process that began in 1817 when the American Colonization Society established a settlement of freed American slaves in what has become the city of Monrovia—the capital of Liberia, named after President James Monroe. Eventually, approximately 11,000 freed slaves emigrated to Liberia. Ironically, many of them perceived their mission to be one of "civilizing" the Africans they would encounter. The descendants of these freed slaves, who are called Americo-Liberians, retain much of the political and economic power in Liberia although they constitute a minority of the population. The other ethnic groups in Liberia include the Kpelle, Bassa, Gio, Kru, Grebo, Mano, and Krahn. In a sense, then, the Americo-Liberians established relationships with native Africans that resembled the relationships established by European colonialists in other parts of Africa.

Although the American Colonization Society may be perceived as progressive in that it established a nation for freed slaves, contemporary scholars generally perceive the organization as conservative since it assumed that blacks could not reside successfully in the United States unless they were slaves. (In later years some African Americans, under the leadership of Marcus Garvey, reached a similar conclusion and also created a back-to-Africa movement.) Because Liberia was established with American assistance for former American residents—even if they had not been treated as true citizens in the United States—European countries did not attempt to colonize Liberia.

Liberia's political and economic structures retain traces of American influence. The medium of exchange is the Liberian dollar, and until a coup in 1980 its constitution resembled the U.S. Constitution. The Liberian flag is red, white, and blue, with a star and stripes. The United States remains one of its primary trading partners, and although political considerations have shifted dramatically since other African countries achieved independence during the 1960s, Liberia continues to receive substantial economic assistance from the United States.

Nigeria

Joseph Asagai, the character most responsible for the subplot relating to Africa and African Americans in *A Raisin in the Sun*, is a citizen of Nigeria and has high hopes for the future of his country. The play is set during the period when Nigeria is working toward independence but has not yet actually achieved it. However, during the late 1950s most politicians and cultural leaders understood that independence for African colonies of European nations was increasingly inevitable. During the decade that followed the first production of the play, nearly every African country did become independent.

Nigeria became independent in 1960. It had been an English colony since 1914, although the Royal Niger Company, an English corporation that was formed as a result of the Berlin Conference, had controlled the region since 1886. Previously the Atlantic coast of Nigeria had been frequented by slave traders. Nigeria spans a large area in part because England, as a colonial power, had insistently expanded its territory as a defense against encroachment from German and French colonies. Despite this fact Nigeria never attracted many white settlers, unlike some other African regions. Subsequent to independence Nigeria suffered frequent political unrest, often stemming from ethnic conflict. From 1967 to 1970, Nigeria experienced a bloody civil war after the Ibos, an ethnic group residing primarily in the eastern region of the country, seceded to form the country of Biafra. Biafra and Nigeria were reunited at the war's end. These ethnic cultures had existed separately for thousands of years prior to European colonization, so any attempt to rule the nation as a single entity was destined to create conflict. The Nok culture in what is now central Nigeria began smelting iron approximately 2,000 years ago, as the character Beneatha informs George Murchison when he insults African culture as "grass huts" (81). In the play Joseph Asagai is a member of the Yoruba tribe, which traditionally lived in the southwestern region of Nigeria. The Yoruba culture developed most significantly between the seventeenth and nineteenth centuries.

For most of the time since independence Nigeria has been ruled by a military government, although a civilian government controlled the country between 1979 and 1984. Today Nigeria is among the most populous (25% of all Africans are Nigerian) and powerful of African nations, in part because of its oil resources. It participates in OPEC (the Organization of Petroleum Exporting Countries), although its own priorities have at times been in conflict with those of other oil-producing nations. Nigeria depends on the income from its oil sales for much of its economic development. However, economic disparity among its citizens remains wide, for although the per capita income is approximately $760, Lagos, the capital, is often considered the most expensive city in the world. Moreover, Nigeria is plagued by the repression of such rights as freedom of speech and of the press, as demonstrated by the government's execution of writer Ken Saro-Wiwa in 1995, an event that elicited international protest. Although he was accused of inciting murder, many people believe he was executed because of his outspoken support of minority rights.

The following documents provide a context for many relational issues among Africans and African Americans and between Africa and the United States. First are excerpts from two articles written during the period when African countries were beginning to achieve independence. These articles examine the importance of independence from an African American perspective. They are followed by excerpts from two books written by white travelers in Africa—an English woman who journeyed through western Africa during the late nineteenth century, and an American journalist who spent considerable time in several African nations during the late 1970s. The next group of documents consists of historically important texts by or about three men—Booker T. Washington, W.E.B. Du Bois, and Marcus Garvey—who had a profound influence on the status of African Americans in the United States and on the relationships among African Americans and Africans.

PHAON GOLDMAN

Phaon Goldman, a writer and historian, begins by discrediting popular stereotypes of Africa similar to the stereotype of Tarzan that Beneatha warns Mama against in *A Raisin in the Sun*. He implies that African Americans have internalized these stereotypes and hence occasionally feel shame at their ancestry. This shame is made worse by the history of American slavery, because some people suggest that Africans permitted themselves to be sold into slavery. In contrast, Goldman lists some of the desperate means by which Africans sought to avoid or escape slavery. He argues that African Americans should be proud of, rather than embarrassed by, their ancestry.

Subsequently Goldman links the situation of many African countries at the beginning of the 1960s with the situation of African Americans in the United States. African Americans ought to use Africans as their models, he suggests, and insist on their own civil rights in the United States. Freedom is a particularly American value, he maintains, and African Americans will achieve a greater sense of dignity if they demand equal treatment in this country that so espouses freedom.

FROM PHAON GOLDMAN, "THE SIGNIFICANCE OF AFRICAN
FREEDOM FOR THE NEGRO AMERICAN"
(The Negro History Bulletin, 1960)

Africa is significant not only because it's in the news, but also because we have an ancestral connection with the peoples of Africa—a connection we need to review and re-appraise. We have only heard since we were wee tots about Africa in terms of the exotic, the outlandish—land of cannibals, slithering snakes, and people who go around boiling missionaries in a pot. . . .

There is also another instance of our background and connection with Africa which we have come to see only in one light, and that is our outlook on the system of slavery—the instrument that brought us to these shores. When we think of slavery we too often visualize happy-go-lucky slaves captured easily and without a struggle. But the truth of the matter is that the Portuguese, Dutch, and British fought many a pitched battle to capture most of the Africans that were taken into slavery. Those men, sold into the chains of the European slave-traders by other Africans, were most often warriors who had been captured in inter-village battles. Tens of thousands of these men died by their own hand on the long middle passage rather than submit to that day's form of man's inhumanity to man. So you can see that our ancestors represent not a bunch of cringing cowards but the most valiant of men in body and spirit. (2)

• • •

So to sum up, with Africa in the news every day we must re-view our past concepts of Africa and our relations with the African people, we must view their current battle for "Freedom Now" through the pressures of boycotts, strikes, and mass protests as that stage of man's eternal quest for human dignity that brings the issues out into the open and forces a decision. We must keep ever in mind that the cry of "Freedom Now" is but the present-day application of the ideas of men like Thomas Jefferson and Patrick Henry whose cry of "Give me liberty or give me death" brought freedom to this country and still inspires men to fight for freedom around the world.

Perhaps the greatest significance of African freedom for the Negro American is that it may light the way for those of us of African descent here in America to re-vitalize America's conscience by moving together now for our freedom and force America to solve her moral dilemma of the race question and resume her rightful place as a world leader by showing in deed as well as in preachment that she is truly the land of "liberty and justice for all." (6)

EARL E. THORPE

Earl E. Thorpe, who was a professor at Southern University in Baton Rouge, Louisiana, also refers to the shame African Americans feel at their African ancestry, and he also urges them to overcome this emotion. He suggests that the most effective way to acquire pride in Africa is to become more educated about African cultures and history. In doing so, he contextualizes the historic relationship between Africa and African Americans. During the nineteenth century, when Liberia was settled by former slaves, many slaves dreamed of returning to Africa. Free blacks in the United States, however, often insisted on their status as Americans—their ancestors might have arrived from Africa, but they were no more African than many white Americans were English or German.

By the early twentieth century, however, many African Americans had become disillusioned with their treatment in the United States. Men like W.E.B. Du Bois and Marcus Garvey believed that emigration to Africa was desirable because African Americans would never achieve equality in the United States. Although their movements attained some popularity, they were short-lived; African Americans effectively ignored Africa until the 1950s and 1960s. Thorpe provides a succinct description of the relationships among these movements and periods.

FROM EARL E. THORPE, "AFRICA IN THE THOUGHT OF NEGRO
AMERICANS"
(*The Negro History Bulletin*, 1959)

In the early decades of the nineteenth century, the work of the American Colonization Society and the founding of Liberia projected Africa into the thought of Negroes in America as never before. Through an analysis of the slave songs, Miles Fisher shows that many slaves became possessed by the dream and hope of being freed and sent to Africa. He believes that many spirituals seem to indicate this dream and hope through references to ships, captains, and sailing [and] were composed during this period. . . .

But if the slave regarded expatriation to Africa as a welcome eventuality, the majority of free Negroes, many of whom were active abolitionists, did not share this attitude. Through mass meetings, orations, petitions, editorials, letters, and other means they remonstrated against the effort to remove them from the United States. Yet the free Negroes revealed ambivalence in their attitude toward Africa. When they were describing the kidnapping of their forebearers from the ancestral home and the horrors of the slave trade, they painted the continent and its people in beautiful glowing terms, but when efforts were made to force free Negroes to "return" to Africa, the overwhelming majority refused to go there and depicted Africa and its people in a quite different light. (7)

• • •

After the brief flurry of talk in the 1880s and 1890s about emigration to Africa, and a mild protest against late nineteenth century imperialism, Afro-American interest in the so-called "Dark Continent" appears to have subsided until the 1920s, when, coincident with the Harlem or Negro Renaissance, interest in Africa burgeoned anew. W.E.B. Du Bois led in the sponsorship of meetings designed to bring Negroid peoples closer together. The first Pan-African Congress, held in Paris in 1919, resulted when Du Bois was sent to Europe by the National Association for the Advancement of Colored People to investigate the treatment of tan G.I.'s. He used this opportunity to organize the Congress, which was attended by fifty-seven delegates from the United States of America, the West Indies, and Africa. Racial concord and advancement were the primary objectives. In 1921 a second Pan-African Congress was held which drew 113 delegates to Europe, two years later a third was held, and the last Congress met in New York City in 1927. (8)

• • •

The movement of the 1920s with which the West Indian immigrant Marcus Garvey has been prominently identified, revolved around an organization called the Universal Improvement Association. Centered in the North, though by no means limited to it, this movement had its genesis in the World War I stimulus to the desire for equality. But while it originated out of the desire for a full share in democracy, the movement really fed on the lynchings and racial strife which characterized the twenties, and on the growing maturity of the race. Sharing the pessimism and disillusionment, as well as the optimism of the period, Marcus Garvey became convinced that the position of his race within the United States was eternally without hope. . . . (9)

Indeed, a dominant characteristic of the mid-twentieth century Negro vis-a-vis Africa is the greatly increased number who have visited that continent, many under auspices of the Point Four and other federally sponsored programs. This travel is helping to dispel much of the ignorance about Africa and Africans which has been evident among Negro Americans. Thus many of the old stereotypes once commonly accepted are now rapidly being discarded. . . . (10)

As a consequence of the degradation of slavery, Negroes have been unique among Americans in the rejection of the land of their fathers. Now a greater maturity and developing race pride are bringing an end to this rejection, and it would not be surprising, to the present writer at least, to see the masses of Afro-Americans soon embrace Africa with a force comparable to that which the Irish and Jewish Americans show for the lands of their fathers. (22)

MARY KINGSLEY

The history of colonialism is essentially the history of white presence in Africa. In some regions Europeans settled and established permanent residences and personal lives, whereas in other regions Europeans established only trade, exploiting the continent for its natural resources. By the end of the nineteenth century, many more wealthy Europeans traveled to Africa as tourists looking for adventure. Mary Kingsley was one such traveler.

Kingsley traveled to West Africa—which had not yet been organized into the countries we know today but which included what would eventually become Nigeria—after the death of her parents. Her espoused reason for traveling to Africa was an attempt to discover unknown animals, especially fish, a task at which she was somewhat successful. At that time it was unusual for a woman to travel alone in Africa, that is, without the protection of a European man.

In this passage she describes a group of Africans with whom she spent considerable time and for whom she apparently felt some affection. Her tone, however, is condescending, particularly to contemporary ears. She refers to many stereotypes of Africans, including the thought that they are cannibals, a worry she expresses throughout her narrative although all her evidence is merely rumor. Throughout this passage Kingsley's assumption is that the Africans are markedly inferior to the Europeans.

FROM MARY KINGSLEY, *TRAVELS IN WEST AFRICA*
(Everyman Classic, 1987 [first published 1897])

They [the Fans, or Fauns, an ethnic group] rarely occupy one site for a village for any considerable time on account—firstly, of their wasteful method of collecting rubber by cutting down the vine, which soon stamps it out of a district; and, secondly, from their quarrelsome ways. So when a village of Fans has cleared all the rubber out of its district, or has made the said district too hot to hold it by rows with other villages, or has got itself very properly shelled out and burnt for some attack on traders or the French flag in any form, its inhabitants clear off into another district, and build another village; for bark and palm thatch are cheap, and house removing just nothing; when you are an unsophisticated cannibal Fan you don't require a pantechnicon van [a furniture moving van] to stow away your one or two mushroom-shaped stools, knives, and cooking-pots, and a calabash [a utensil made from a hollow gourd] or so.

If you are rich, maybe you will have a box with clothes in as well, but as a general rule all your clothes are on your back. So your wives just pick up the stools and the knives and the cooking-pots, and the box, and the children toddle off with the calabashes. You have, of course, the gun to carry, for sleeping or waking a Fan never parts with his gun. . . . Now and again, for lack of immediate neighbouring villages to quarrel with, one end of a village will quarrel with the other end. The weaker end then goes off and builds itself another village, keeping an eye lifting for any member of the stronger end who may come conveniently into its neighbourhood to be killed and eaten. (49–50)

DAVID LAMB

David Lamb bases much of his information about Africa on his experiences working as a journalist in several African nations during the 1970s. By the end of his time there he had grown pessimistic regarding the possibility that African governments would ever be organized and democratic enough to provide for their people. Nevertheless his tone is much more neutral than Kingsley's, and he synthesizes a wealth of information.

In the passages that follow he provides a description of the continent in general, drawing several comparisons so that American readers will have a better understanding of the enormity and diversity of the continent. There is one weakness in this description: he frequently compares the continent of Africa with individual European or North American countries; hence Africa's problems loom much larger. A better strategy would have been to compare the continent of Africa with the continent of Europe rather than with a single country such as Belgium. Yet Lamb's strategy illustrates the fact that many Americans do consider Africa a single unit rather than several dozen distinct nations.

Subsequently the excerpt focuses on Nigeria. Lamb provides a historical analysis of the country, much of which confirms the assertions made by Beneatha Younger and Joseph Asagai in *A Raisin in the Sun.*

FROM DAVID LAMB, *THE AFRICANS*
(Random House, 1982)

If Africa is much discussed and little understood these days, it is hardly surprising, for the continent is as diverse and complex as it is huge. Africa is four times larger than the United States and has twice as many people. It spans seven time zones, and to fly from Nairobi in the east to Dakar, Senegal, in the west takes longer than to fly from New York to London. It is inhabited by 2,000 tribes or ethnic groups, most of which have a specific language or dialect. In many capitals you can have lunch with an Oxford-educated businessman who wears three-piece Western suits and asks you about last year's Super Bowl game, then drive a few hours and dine on a recently slaughtered goat with illiterate herdsmen who hunt with bows and arrows, live on a barter economy and think all white men are missionaries or doctors. (xiii)

• • •

The Portuguese, in the fifteenth century, were the first Europeans to undertake systemic voyages of discovery southward along the African coast. Thus began six centuries of contact between African and European in which the African—until recently, when he learned how to turn the white man's feelings of guilt into a gold mine of international aid—always ended up second best. The Portuguese explorers opened the door for the slave traders, who in turn ushered in the missionaries, who were, in their own right, agents of colonialism. Each invader—slaver, missionary, colonialist—sought to exploit and convert. Each came to serve himself or his God, not the African. With Europe looking for new markets and materials during the industrial revolution of the nineteenth century, the European powers scrambled for domination in Africa, Balkanizing [dividing an area into small, hostile units] the continent into colonies with artificial boundaries that ignored traditional ethnic groupings. By 1920 every square inch of Africa except Ethiopia, Liberia and the Union of South Africa was under European rule or protection or was claimed by a European country. (8–9)

• • •

The ethnic diversity of Africa also creates an immense language problem, making Africa the most linguistically complex continent in the world. Canada's national unity is fractured by the presence of just two languages. Belgium is splintered by French and Flemish. But Africa, in addition to half a dozen imported European languages, speaks 750 tribal tongues, fifty of which are spoken by one million or more people. Both Swahili in East Africa and Hausa in West Africa are spoken by more than 25 million people. In Zaire alone, there are seventy-five different languages. In South Africa the whites speak Afrikaans, a colloquial form of seventeenth-century Dutch heard nowhere else in the world. The tribal babble intellectually cripples whole countries and leaves Africa in the unenviable position of not being able to understand itself. (14)

• • •

Trapped by its colonial past, divided by political and cultural differences, isolated by the absence of an intra-Africa highway or an intra-Africa communications system, each country is little more than a haphazardly placed economic pocket, neither related to nor dependent on its neighbors. As a group of three or four major regional communities, Africa could have great economic strength. As fifty-one separate entities, it has virtually none.

The colonialists' introduction of export-crop farming had moved the African peasant from a barter to a cash economy. But the countryside could not provide the wages and jobs families needed, so men left their farms—and their wives and mothers—and drifted into the cities where the money and the work were. There they found that the promises of the cities were mostly an illusion. Governments nationalized private enterprises, resulting in economic stagnation, and presidents preached a doctrine of economic socialism without understanding socialistic theory or daring to give workers control of state power. Economies could not expand fast enough to absorb the job seekers and many young, talented Africans went off to Europe and the United States to study and work, depriving Africa of some of its brightest minds. (289–90)

• • •

Nigeria is as large as California, Arizona and New Mexico combined. It has 250 ethnic groups, which speak a hundred different languages. Its coastal mangrove swamps extend to the wooded savannah of the central plateau and finally give way to the northern deserts, as barren and Godforsaken as the Sahara. Its cities are overcrowded and unmanageable, with slums and suburbs competing for the same turf, and Oxford-educated millionaires and unemployed illiterates sharing the same block. Contrasts and contradictions are everywhere. And everywhere there is a reminder that Nigeria moves to the rhythm of money, big money that springs from its plentiful oil wells. Nigeria is the Brazil of Africa. It is a country that has come alive and made things happen, even though it is far from immune to the problems that haunt every African nation.

Part of what makes Nigeria different from the rest of black Africa is its history, for it is no cultural upstart. The Noks were casting iron and producing terra-cotta sculpture before the birth of Christ. The northern cities of Kano and Katsina were cosmopolitan terminals on the trans-Sahara caravan routes when William the Conqueror ruled England. And when the first Europeans reached Benin in the fifteenth century—a good many years before Columbus set off for the Americas—they found a highly organized kingdom with a disciplined army, an elaborate ceremonial court, and artisans whose work in ivory, bronze, wood and brass is prized throughout the world today for its craftsmanship and beauty.

The first whites to reach Nigeria were Portuguese explorers. Then came the traders, who bought strong young Nigerians for $4 each from local chiefs—the slaves sold for up to $130 apiece at auctions in the Americas—and the missionaries. The European powers recognized Britain's claim to Nigeria at the Berlin Conference and the London-based Royal Niger Company was chartered to develop commercial ties. The British government took over the company's territory in 1900, and fourteen years later the area was formally united as the Colony and Protectorate of Nigeria. (Administratively Nigeria remained divided into the Northern and Southern provinces and Lagos Colony.)

By African standards Nigeria was an advanced society, and the British, realizing its economic potential, tried to make sure that it would develop as a truly *black* colony. There were fewer than 12,000 Europeans in Nigeria's pre-independence population of 32 million, and no white man was allowed to enter Nigeria, much less work there, unless he could prove that his presence was necessary. Whites were not allowed to settle or buy businesses, and everyone who did enter had to post a sizable bond. Interestingly, the British seldom referred to the local population as "natives." They called the people what they were, "Nigerians," a mark of respect seen in almost no other colony. As far back as 1922, the British permitted African legislators to be included in a council for Lagos Colony and the Southern Province. In 1943 the British appointed three Africans to the Nigerian Executive Council, which was under the jurisdiction of the British Governor's Cabinet. By the end of World War II, Britain was moving Nigeria toward self-government on a representative, federal basis. The reason was more self-serving than altruistic: London did not want to risk losing Nigeria as a member of the Commonwealth when independence inevitably came.

In October 1960 Nigeria passed, peacefully and uneventfully, from colonialism to nationhood. The enterprise of black traders and business men, based on cocoa and palm-oil exports, was well established by then. There was, however small, an educated African middle class, a lively black press that had been functioning for more than a hundred years, an active parliament, a sturdy economy and an agricultural sector that produced enough food to feed the nation. Nigeria even had five hundred black doctors, a remarkable number considering that many new countries started off with none. On top of that, four years earlier, drillers had discovered deep pools of oil in the Niger delta. Even nature, it seemed, had smiled on Nigeria.

But black Africa's biggest hope soon became its greatest disappointment. In the first sixteen years of independence there were three coups d'état, the assassinations of two heads of state, and one civil war that claimed a million lives. The country's oil revenues were squandered in the biggest spending binge any African country ever went on. The soldiers came to power and proved themselves more corrupt and less efficient than the civilians they had overthrown for their corruption and inefficiency. The cities filled up and broke down. The farmlands emptied and stopped producing. The parliament dissolved, the economy deteriorated, the dreams disintegrated.

With many African countries, you could end the story right there. But not with Nigeria. It did what no other African country had been able to do: reverse the downward skid, revert from military to civilian rule and recapture some of the promises that independence was all about. For Nigeria, the 1980s brought membership in an exclusive club of one. It was emerging as black Africa's first mini-power, a nation with enough clout to influence policy in capitals from Washington to Moscow. It is the one black country in Africa whose future really matters to the outside world, and the one country whose present is described in superlatives. (299–301)

BOOKER T. WASHINGTON

In *A Raisin in the Sun*, Mama and Mrs. Johnson have a brief argument about the philosophy of Booker T. Washington; the argument concludes with Mama referring to him as a fool. Washington is a figure who has consistently evoked a divided response. Some have seen him as most helpful because he was most practical, whereas others have seen him as most harmful because he was most cautious. He did not urge his followers to demand absolutely equal rights, but rather to make the most of their situation.

In the excerpt from his "Atlanta Constitution Address" of 1901,

Washington relies on an extended metaphor: "cast down your bucket where you are." He means that African Americans should rely on the economic opportunities they have, even if those opportunities are limited to service jobs. He suggests that more abstract education will provide African Americans with nothing but dissatisfaction. Although he acknowledges the history of slavery, he urges former slaves and their children and grandchildren to be content with beginning at the bottom and working their way up, as if their generations in slavery did not involve meaningful work. In this sense, Washington was assimilationist rather than radical. As the conversation between Mama and Mrs. Younger demonstrates, Washington remained influential long after he delivered this address. African Americans took many of his suggestions seriously well into the twentieth century. He continues to be acknowledged as a significant figure even among those who disagree with his ideas.

FROM BOOKER T. WASHINGTON, "THE ATLANTA CONSTITUTION ADDRESS"
(Penguin, 1986 [originally published 1901])

To those of my race who depend on bettering their condition in a foreign land or who underestimate the importance of cultivating friendly relations with the Southern white man, who is their next-door neighbour, I would say: "Cast down your bucket where you are"—cast it down in making friends in every manly way of the people of all races by whom we are surrounded.

Cast it down in agriculture, mechanics, in commerce, in domestic service, and in the professions. And in this connection it is well to bear in mind that whatever other sins the South may be called to bear, when it comes to business, pure and simple, it is in the South that the Negro is given a man's chance in the commercial world, and in nothing is this Exposition more eloquent than in emphasizing this chance. Our greatest danger is that in the great leap from slavery to freedom we may overlook the fact that the masses of us are to live by the productions of our hands, and fail to keep in mind that we shall prosper in proportion as we learn to dignify and glorify common labour and put brains and skill into the common occupations of life; shall prosper in proportion as we learn to draw the line between the superficial and the substantial, the ornamental gewgaws of life and the useful. No race can prosper till it learns that there is as much dignity in tilling a field as in writing a poem. It is at the bottom of life we must begin, and not at the top. Nor should we permit our grievances to overshadow our opportunities. (219–20)

W.E.B. DU BOIS

W.E.B. Du Bois is often positioned in opposition to Booker T. Washington, in part because he represented the liberally educated class of blacks that Washington discouraged. Early in his career Du Bois attempted to reconcile his identity as a black man and as an American—although later he emigrated to Ghana as a result of his disillusionment with race relations in the United States. In the section of *The Souls of Black Folk* excerpted here, Du Bois describes his sense of self in a phrase that has become famous: "double-consciousness." Through this phrase he acknowledges that African Americans are seldom seen as individuals by white Americans but rather are classified simply as members of their race. According to Du Bois, African Americans realize this situation and therefore can never be completely unself-conscious anywhere in the United States. Du Bois founded the National Association for the Advancement of Colored People (NAACP) and served as editor of its newspaper, *The Crisis*. In his most well-known book, *The Souls of Black Folk*, originally published in 1903, he predicts that the issue of race will dominate the twentieth century in the United States.

FROM W.E.B. DU BOIS, *THE SOULS OF BLACK FOLK*
(Bantam, 1989 [first published 1903])

. . . the Negro is a sort of seventh son, born with a veil, and gifted with second-sight in this American world—a world which yields him no true self-consciousness, but only lets him see himself through the revelation of the other world. It is a peculiar sensation, this double-consciousness, this sense of always looking at one's self through the eyes of others, of measuring one's soul by the tape of a world that looks on in amused contempt and pity. One ever feels his twoness—an American, a Negro; two souls, two thoughts, two unreconciled strivings; two warring ideals in one dark body, whose dogged strength alone keeps it from being torn asunder.

The history of the American Negro is the history of this strife—this longing to attain self-conscious manhood, to merge his double self into a better and truer self. In this merging he wishes neither of the older selves to be lost. He would not Africanize America, for America has too much to teach the world and Africa. He would not bleach his Negro soul in a flood of white Americanism, for he knows that Negro blood has a message for the world. He simply wishes to make it possible for a man to be both a Negro and an American, without being cursed and spit upon by his fellows, without having the doors of Opportunity closed roughly in his face. (2–3)

POLITICAL JOURNALISM DURING THE EARLY TWENTIETH CENTURY

Several newspapers and magazines were published for an African American audience during the early decades of the twentieth century. Large cities usually had a newspaper aimed specifically at a black audience—as they do today. These newspapers and magazines provided a forum for debates within the community. Marcus Garvey and W.E.B. Du Bois, among others, frequently published editorials and articles in these periodicals, thereby attaining a national voice. Garvey wrote most often for the *Negro World*, whereas Du Bois wrote for the *Crisis*, the journal affiliated with the NAACP and edited by Du Bois, who was among the founders of the organization.

These articles occasionally displayed rancor as the two men competed for dominance within the African American community, although Garvey claims (in the article that follows immediately) that the two are not rivals.

GARVEY'S "WHAT GARVEY THINKS OF DU BOIS"

As this article demonstrates, personal attacks found their way into the publications that Garvey and Du Bois used as vehicles for debate. Garvey distinguishes between the NAACP and the UNIA (Universal Negro Improvement Association), which he headed, by claiming that the NAACP appeals only to upper-class and well-educated African Americans—certainly a small group—whereas the UNIA appeals to working-class, practical-minded African Americans. In this sense he seems to agree with Booker T. Washington in the complaints he registers against Du Bois.

FROM MARCUS GARVEY, "WHAT GARVEY THINKS OF DU BOIS"
(*Negro World*, 1921) [Reprinted in *Voices of a Black Nation*, ed.
Theodore G. Vincent]

A brilliant student of sociology, a literary genius, a man of letters, Dr. Du Bois could grace a chair in any university in the world, but when it comes to mingling with men and dealing with practical affairs, he sometimes strikes the wrong note. . . .

As we study the personality of Dr. Du Bois, we find that he only appreciates one type of men, and that is the cultured, refined type which lingers around universities and attends pink tea affairs. The men of dynamic force of the Negro race, the men with ability to sway and move the masses, Dr. Du Bois cannot appraise at their face value, and that is why the author of the "Souls of Black Folk," while the idol of the drawing room aristocrats, could not thus far become the popular leader of the masses of his own race. (97–98)

• • •

. . . Du Bois appeals to the "Talented Tenth," while Garvey appeals to the "Oi Polloi." The NAACP appeals to the Beau Brummell, Lord Chesterfield, kid gloved, silk stocking, creased trousers, patent leather shoe, Bird of Paradise hat and Hudson seal coat with beaver or skunk collar element, while the UNIA appeals to the sober, sane, serious, earnest, hard-working man, who earns his living by the sweat of his brow. The NAACP appeals to the cavalier element in the Negro race, while the UNIA appeals to the self-reliant yeomanry. Hence, in no sense are Dr. Du Bois and Mr. James Weldon Johnson rivals of Marcus Garvey. Du Bois and Johnson as writers and speakers and Garvey as prophet, propagandist and organizer and inspirer of the masses are doing good work and all should be free and unimpeded in perfecting their plans. (98)

DU BOIS'S "AFRICA FOR THE AFRICANS"

In this article Du Bois attempts to accomplish two somewhat contradictory tasks. First, he argues for the end of colonialism in Africa—but on African terms. According to Du Bois, Europeans, though they claim to instill order in Africa, actually only exploit its natural resources for their own financial benefit. Therefore, Europeans should not influence the partition of Africa. Within this section Du Bois groups people of African descent, including African Americans, with Africans. He maintains that if an African American desires to emigrate to Africa, that person should do so with the expectation that he or she could succeed financially and socially. Such a choice, however, should be entirely voluntary.

Second, Du Bois vehemently states that African Americans are in fact Americans. The ancestors of many African Americans arrived in North America long before the ancestors of many white Americans did. Through their labor, he believes, African Americans have contributed to the economic development of the United States and deserve to share in its success.

FROM W.E.B. DU BOIS, "AFRICA FOR THE AFRICANS"
(*Crisis*, 1919) [Reprinted in *Voices of a Black Nation*, ed. Theodore
G. Vincent]

The truth is, white men are merely juggling with words—or worse—when they declare that the withdrawal of Europeans from Africa will plunge that continent into chaos. What Europe, and indeed only a small group in Europe, wants in Africa is not a field for the spread of European civilization, but a field for exploitation. They covet the raw materials—ivory, diamonds, copper and rubber in which the land abounds, and even more do they covet cheap native labor to mine and produce these things. Greed—naked, pitiless lust for wealth and power, lie back of all of Europe's interest in Africa and the white world knows it and is not ashamed.

Any readjustment of Africa is not fair and cannot be lasting which does not consider the interests of native Africans and peoples of African descent. Prejudice, in European colonies in Africa, against the ambitious Negro is greater than in America, and that is saying much. But with the establishment of a form of government which shall be based on the concept that Africa is for Africans, there would be a chance for the colored American to emigrate and to go as a pioneer to a country which must, sentimentally at least, possess for him the same fascination as England does for Indian-born Englishmen.

This is not a "separatist" movement. There is no need to think that those who advocate the opening up of Africa for Africans and those of African descent desire to deport any large number of colored Americans to a foreign and, in some respects, inhospitable land. Once for all, let us realize that we are Americans, that we were brought here with the earliest settlers, and that the very sort of civilization from which we came made the complete adoption of western modes and customs imperative if we were to survive at all. In brief, there is nothing so indigenous, so completely "made in America" as we. It is as absurd to talk of a return to Africa, merely because that was our home 300 years ago, as it would be to expect the members of the Caucasian race to return to the vastnesses of the Caucuses Mountains from which, it is reputed, they sprang. (269–70)

GARVEY'S "THE AFRICAN REPUBLIC AND WHITE POLITICS"

In this article Garvey clarifies his stance regarding the United States and Africa. He claims that he is not an anarchist or radical, terms that held much power in the United States during the early 1920s because the Russian Revolution had recently occurred and many Americans had begun to fear communism and other frequently misunderstood political philosophies. Yet, Garvey claims, in relation to Africa he is a radical. He urges Africans and people of African descent to eliminate white residents from the continent, by force if necessary. The wealth, land, and labor of Africa have been stolen, he asserts, and justice demands that Africa be reclaimed for Africans.

FROM MARCUS GARVEY, "THE AFRICAN REPUBLIC AND WHITE
POLITICS"
(*Negro World*, 1921) [Reprinted in *Voices of a Black Nation*, ed.
Theodore G. Vincent]

Africa must be redeemed. There is no doubt about it, it is no camouflage. The Universal Negro Improvement Association is organizing now, and there is going to be some dying later on. We are not organizing to fight against or disrespect the government of America, I say this plainly and for everybody to hear—we are organizing to drive every pale-face out of Africa. . . . Do you know why? Because Africa is mine; Africa is the land of my fathers; and what my fathers never gave to anybody else, since they did not will it to anybody, must have been for me. . . .

If anybody should be a radical it should be the Negro. We are not radicals, even though some men think we are. The I.W.W. [Industrial Workers of the World] are radicals, and so are some Socialists; but they are white people, so let them "raise Cain" and do what they please. We have no time with them; we have all the time with four hundred million Negroes. . . . So, please understand that Marcus Garvey . . . is no anarchist, as far as Western civilization is concerned; but if anarchism means that you have to drive out somebody and sometimes kill somebody, to get that which belongs to you, then when I get to Africa I am going to be an anarchist.

If it is right for the white man and the yellow man to rule in their respective domains, it is right for the black man to rule in his own domain. Remaining here you will never have a black man as president of the United States; you will never have a black Premier of Great Britain; you need not waste time over it. I am going to use all my time to establish a great republic in Africa for four hundred million Negroes, so that one day if I desire to be president, I can throw my hat in the ring and run as a candidate for the presidency. (272–73)

DU BOIS'S "MANIFESTO"

The second Pan-African Congress occurred in September 1921. It was a loosely organized association that had as its primary goal the liberation of Africa from colonialism. Several subsequent congresses occurred throughout the following decades. In this Manifesto, Du Bois summarizes the acts of several European countries that claim colonial territory in Africa. He also critiques the United States for its role in maintaining the colonial status of Africa.

FROM W.E.B. DU BOIS, "MANIFESTO OF THE SECOND PAN-
AFRICAN CONGRESS"
(*Crisis*, 1921) [Reprinted in *Voices of a Black Nation*, ed. Theodore
G. Vincent]

England, with her Pax Brittanica, her courts of justice, established commerce and a certain apparent recognition of native law and customs, has nevertheless systematically fostered ignorance among the natives, has enslaved them and is still enslaving some of them, has usually declined even to try to train black and brown men in real self-government, to recognize civilized black folks as civilized, or to grant to colored colonies those rights of self-government which it freely gives to white men.

Belgium is a nation which has but recently assumed responsibility for her colonies, and has taken some steps to lift them from the worst abuses of the autocratic regime; but she has not confirmed to the people the possession of their land and labor, and she shows no disposition to allow the natives any voice in their own government, or to provide for their political future. Her colonial policy is still mainly dominated by the banks and great corporations. But we are glad to learn that the present government is considering a liberal program of reform for the future.

Portugal and Spain have never drawn a legal cast line against persons of culture who happen to be of Negro descent. Portugal has a humane code for the natives and has begun their education in some regions. But unfortunately, the industrial concessions of Portuguese Africa are almost wholly in the hands of foreigners whom Portugal cannot or will not control, and who are exploiting land and re-establishing the African slave trade.

The United States of America after brutally enslaving millions of black folks suddenly emancipated them and began their education; but it acted without system or forethought, throwing the freed men upon the world penniless and landless, educating them without thoroughness and system, and subjecting them the while to lynching, lawlessness, discrimination, insult and slander, such as human beings have seldom endured and survived. To save their own government, they enfranchised the Negro and then when danger passed, allowed hundreds of thousands of educated and civilized black folk to be lawlessly disfranchised and subjected to a caste system; and, at the same time, in 1776, 1812, 1861, 1897, and 1917, they asked and allowed thousands of black men to offer up their lives as a sacrifice to the country which despised and despises them.

France alone of the great colonial powers has sought to place her cultured black citizens on a plane of absolute legal and social equality with her whites and given them representation in her highest legislature. In her colonies she has a widespread but still imperfect system of state education. This splendid beginning must be completed by widening the political basis of her native government, by restoring to the indigenes [those who were native to the place] the ownership of the soil, by protecting native labor against the aggression of established capital, and by asking no man, black or white, to be a soldier unless the country gives him a voice in his own government. (281–83)

MALCOLM X AND MARCUS GARVEY

In this opening section of his autobiography, Malcolm X, a leader of the civil rights movement during early 1960s, traces his investment in civil rights to his family history. Although Marcus Garvey sometimes seems to fade into history as many Americans associate the civil rights movement most strongly with leaders like Malcolm X and Martin Luther King, Malcolm X here asserts the continuity of the movement. In other words, the 1960s are not that far removed from the 1920s. Garvey could be perceived as dangerous not simply because he urged African Americans to return to Africa (though any removal of such a contingent of the working class would have had devastating effects on the American economy) but because Garvey's movement indicated that African Americans could unite themselves and hence achieve political and economic power rather than simply be controlled by more dominant groups. Ironically, until his assassination in 1965, Malcolm X was also viewed by some as the most dangerous black man in America.

FROM MALCOLM X, *THE AUTOBIOGRAPHY OF MALCOLM X*
(Random House, 1964)

When my mother was pregnant with me, she told me later, a party of hooded Ku Klux Klan riders galloped up to our home in Omaha, Nebraska, one night. Surrounding the house, brandishing their shotguns and rifles, they shouted for my father to come out. My mother went to the front door and opened it. Standing where they could see her pregnant condition, she told them that she was alone with her three small children, and that my father was away, preaching, in Milwaukee. The Klansmen shouted threats and warnings at her that we had better get out of town because "the good Christian white people" were not going to stand for my father's "spreading trouble" among the "good" Negroes of Omaha with the "back to Africa" preachings of Marcus Garvey.

My father, the Reverend Earl Little, was a Baptist minister, a dedicated organizer for Marcus Aurelius Garvey's U.N.I.A. (Universal Negro Improvement Association). With the help of such disciples as my father, Garvey, from his headquarters in New York City's Harlem, was raising the banner of black-race purity and exhorting the Negro masses to return to their ancestral African homeland—a cause which had made Garvey the most controversial black man on earth.

• • •

. . . He [Earl Little] believed, as did Marcus Garvey, that freedom, independence and self-respect could never be achieved by the Negro in America, and that therefore the Negro should leave America to the white man and return to his African land of origin. (1–2)

TOPICS FOR WRITTEN OR ORAL EXPLORATION

1. Read a biography and write an essay about the life of a prominent individual in the civil rights movement. Examples include W.E.B. Du Bois, Marcus Garvey, Booker T. Washington, Rosa Parks, Martin Luther King, Malcolm X, Medgar Evers, and Ida B. Wells.

2. Read a biography and write an essay about the life of an African leader. Examples include Haile Selassie, Leopold-Sedar Senghor, Kwame Nkrumah, Anwar al-Sadat, Bishop Desmond Tutu, and Nelson Mandela.

3. Choose one African nation and research its history. Focus on a particular time period, for example, the era before colonization, the late nineteenth century or the 1960s.

4. In your class, debate the advantages and disadvantages of assimilation. Why would a person hope to assimilate? Why would a person object to assimilation?

5. Write an essay tracing the use of the term "African American." Analyze the racial terms that preceded it, and discuss the factors contributing to as well as the effects of such shifting terminology.

6. Discuss whether "dreams" are presented as positive or negative forces in the play *A Raisin in the Sun*. Compare the "dreams" aspired to by characters in this play with Martin Luther King's "I Have a Dream" speech and with Anne Moody's critique of that speech at the end of her autobiography, *Coming of Age in Mississippi* (1968).

7. In an essay, compare Mama's and Beneatha's attitudes toward Africa.

8. Research the effects of missionaries on African countries or regions. In what ways did missionaries achieve their goals? In what ways were the goals of the missionaries compatible with or dependent on the military or economic goals of European countries? What does Beneatha imply about the relationship between missionary activity and colonialism?

9. Analyze Mama's comment that the meaning of life once lay in freedom, but today the meaning of life is found in money. Do you think this is an accurate perception of the African American community? To what extent can it be extended to American culture in general? (See page 74 of *A Raisin in the Sun*.)

10. Look up the terms "assimilationist" and "Uncle Tom." Analyze the character of George. Is he an assimilationist or an Uncle Tom?

11. Read further in Booker T. Washington's *Up from Slavery* (1901).

Would you agree with Mrs. Johnson that he is a hero, or with Mama that he is a fool?

12. Beneatha predicts that future political leaders of African countries will be as corrupt as colonial leaders have been. Based on your knowledge of recent history, discuss whether you think she is correct. (See pages 133–34 of *A Raisin in the Sun*.)

13. Walter states that Travis represents the sixth generation of Youngers in America (148). Research the immigration patterns of another ethnic group and compare that group's presence in America with the presence of African Americans.

14. Read further in Malcolm X's *Autobiography*. Write an essay describing what you believe that book has to say to teen-agers and young adults today.

15. Look up Africa in a history or geography textbook you have used. Write an essay comparing the information given in your textbook to the statements made by Earl E. Thorpe or David Lamb in the excerpts included in this chapter. If differences exist, state which source you choose to believe.

16. Based on the excerpts from their political journalism included in this chapter, Marcus Garvey and W.E.B. Du Bois seem to have had an antagonistic relationship. Yet, they often had similar goals. Reread those articles and identify the points on which the two men agree.

SUGGESTED READINGS

Achebe, Chinua. *Things Fall Apart*. New York: Doubleday, 1958.

Clower, Robert W., et al. *Growth without Development: An Economic Survey of Liberia*. Evanston, IL: Northwestern University Press, 1966.

Davidson, Basil. *Let Freedom Come: Africa in Modern History*. Boston: Atlantic–Little, Brown, 1978.

de St. Jorre, John. *The Brothers' War: Biafra and Nigeria*. New York: Houghton Mifflin, 1972.

Duignan, Peter, and L.H. Gann. *The United States and Africa: A History*. Cambridge: Cambridge University Press, 1984.

Gordimer, Nadine. *A Sport of Nature*. New York: Viking, 1988.

Hibbert, Christopher. *Africa Explored: Europeans in the Dark Continent, 1769–1889*. New York: Norton, 1982.

July, Robert W. *A History of the African People*. New York: Charles Scribner's Sons, 1970.

Melady, Thomas Patrick. *Profiles of African Leaders*. New York: Macmillan, 1961.

Shepherd, George W., Jr. *The Politics of African Nationalism: Challenge to American Policy.* New York: Praeger, 1962.

Soyinka, Wole. *Ake: The Years of Childhood.* New York: Random House, 1983.

Ungar, Sanford J. *Africa: The People and Politics of an Emerging Continent.* New York: Simon and Schuster, 1985.

4

A Raisin in the Sun and the Chicago Literary Tradition

Although people are tempted to read *A Raisin in the Sun* autobiographically because Lorraine Hansberry grew up in Chicago between the two world wars, her circumstances differed significantly from those of the Younger family. However, some incidents in her background probably did contribute to her choice of material in the plays she wrote. In interviews and print, Hansberry has discussed her family's experiences in attempting to integrate a white neighborhood in Chicago, though she more often speaks of her experiences *after* the move. Thus, a more directly autobiographical play might have occurred had Hansberry extended the script and explored the Youngers' lives after they moved to Clybourne Park.

Direct references to the play's setting in Chicago are rare in *A Raisin in the Sun*; the plot could be transported to virtually any major northern city with very few changes. This is not a criticism of the play but rather a comment on the pervasiveness of segregation in American cities during the 1950s. (Segregation in the South may have been or could appear more genteel; that is, not all housing for African Americans was of poor quality there. In the South, Mama's desire to purchase the best house for the best price would not necessarily have implied integration.)

A RAISIN IN THE SUN AND THE CHICAGO SETTING

The first minor reference to the play's setting in Chicago occurs when Walter reads a newspaper article about Colonel McCormick, a man for whom Ruth expresses little sympathy because she believes he is insulated from the problems she experiences. A historical figure, McCormick was a prominent Chicago resident for whom the city's convention center, McCormick Place, has been named. The *Tribune*, which Walter reads, was at the time and is still considered the more reputable of Chicago's newspapers. Later in the scene when Beneatha enters, the stage directions comment on her accent, which has been influenced by her higher education as well as by her midwestern rather than southern upbringing. Nevertheless, the stage directions indicate that her accent is "south side," suggesting that she substitutes the "d" sound for "th," an accent as easy to recognize (and parody) as traditional Brooklynese. In Act Two, scene two, the characters make several additional references to Chicago, generally to criticize white power-brokers; but again, the setting could be moved to a variety of other cities without significant change.

On the other hand, Chicago has often been considered notorious for the intensity of its segregation. More than residents of many other cities, those of Chicago have continued to practice de facto if illegal segregation, though some neighborhoods (particularly those populated by well-educated professionals in newer apartment buildings) have been successfully integrated. The city's public housing projects, including the Robert Taylor Homes on the south side, are crowded, violent, and predominantly black. North of the river the neighborhoods are much more predominantly white. Until recently Chicago city politics were known to be among the most corrupt in the nation, and its public school system remains among the most inadequate. Yet business opportunities for African Americans have increased; no longer would a man like Walter Younger be limited to owning a liquor store, for there are currently more than 10,000 black-owned businesses in Chicago. Of course, this is still a small percentage of all of the businesses owned in the city.

CHICAGO AS AN ECONOMIC HUB

Some of Chicago's racial problems can be traced to historical and geographic coincidence. The city was incorporated in 1837, after the remaining Native Americans were forced west of the Mississippi River and immediately before several surges of European immigration to the United States took place. For example, as a result of the Irish potato famine, which began in 1845, many Irish people immigrated to the United States and a substantial number of them settled in Chicago. Their descendants remain influential in local politics, and St. Patrick's Day in Chicago is virtually a legal holiday. After the Civil War, German and Polish immigrants arrived and established their own neighborhoods. Large numbers of African Americans moved to the city during World War I, when many industries expanded to fill the demands of war. Many of Chicago's neighborhoods have retained their ethnic flavor, a fact that has both positive and negative effects. After all, ethnic diversity can create a rich culture that more homogeneous environments lack, yet this same diversity may contribute to tension among different groups.

Because Chicago is located at the base of Lake Michigan, and because its canal system provides access to the Mississippi River, the city was a transportation hub during the nineteenth century. Its location marked the border between the industrial East and the agricultural West, so it was able to facilitate the exchange of raw materials and manufactured goods between regions. In Hansberry's play, Walter Younger describes this geographic situation after driving to the steel mills of Gary, Indiana, and the dairylands of Wisconsin. Chicago's identity as a border town was especially strong when rail transportation predominated. At this time Chicago was particularly known for its stockyards and grain market. Nearly all cattle and hogs raised in the United States were slaughtered in Chicago; the beef and pork products were then shipped throughout the country. The stockyards closed in 1971.

THE CHICAGO LITERARY TRADITION

Because of Chicago's history and position as one of the few major midwestern cities, it has provided the setting for many works of literature in addition to *A Raisin in the Sun*, as well as a home for many contemporary writers. Several of the novels and stories that rely on Chicago for a setting, especially those written prior to *A Raisin in the Sun*, present the city as a particularly brutal place for poor people or new immigrants.

Although publishing centers in the United States have tended to be located on the east coast, most prominently in New York, and although much classic American literature features New England settings, a literary tradition has also grown up in and around Chicago. As one would expect, the concerns of Chicago writers—and midwestern writers generally—often differ from those of writers from New England or the Deep South. In particular, many writers address the place of Chicago as a major city surrounded by a much more agricultural environment. Because such cities tend to attract people looking for work, the industrial concerns of Chicago are reflected in its literature. Often, this literature takes the form of protest against working and housing conditions or against the plight of the urban poor. Writers, in other words, take on the battles of the urban poor, people who themselves do not have easy access to the mass media, in an attempt to evoke outrage from a national audience. Like many cities at various points in American history, especially when large numbers of immigrants arrived during the nineteenth century, or when rural American citizens migrated to cities during World War II, the population of Chicago grew more quickly than its infrastructure, a fact that contributed to these poor conditions. (Of course, some other pieces of literature, such as *The Great Gatsby* by F. Scott Fitzgerald, present the Midwest as a place from which to escape.) Yet one of the most famous pieces of protest literature, *The Jungle* by Upton Sinclair, a section of which is excerpted here, is set in the meat-packing plants of Chicago.

The documents that follow examine Hansberry's experience in Chicago and representations of Chicago from a variety of perspectives. First, Margaret Wilkerson discusses some of the facts she discovered—and the strategies she used—while researching Hansberry's life. Then Nathan Hare discusses a race riot that occurred in Chicago in 1919, placing that event in the broader context of race relations in this country. The next set of documents feature excerpts from diverse works of classic literature. Three are novels set in Chicago—*Sister Carrie*, *The Jungle*, and *Native Son*. Another is one of Carl Sandburg's most famous poems, which celebrates the city. The other, Jane Addams's *Twenty Years at Hull-House*, is an autobiography primarily concerned with Addams's experience as a social worker during the late nineteenth century.

MARGARET WILKERSON'S "EXCAVATING OUR HISTORY"

In this article Margaret Wilkerson considers the relationships between *A Raisin in the Sun* and Lorraine Hansberry's life. The play is not as autobiographical as some readers might assume, for although Hansberry did grow up in Chicago, and although segregation had a significant influence on her thinking, her family was comparatively privileged economically. For example, Hansberry's family employed a chauffeur—a particularly ironic detail given Walter Younger's frustration with this role. Although slavery would not be as strongly echoed when a black man acts as servant to another black man as it would be when a black man acts as servant to a white man, the position of servant itself remains distinct from independence. Nevertheless, Hansberry suffered the consequences of trying to integrate a previously all-white neighborhood. She experienced the indignity of racial slurs and occasional physical assaults. Like the Youngers, she was forced to confront neighbors who objected to her presence because of her race. Rather than being a haven from her society's racism, her home was instead an object of it. So while the play is not an autobiography, it is informed by Hansberry's personal experience. Her father, Carl Hansberry, pursued the matter as far as the Supreme Court. Althouth he won the case, the justices' ruling was not as broadly applicable as Carl Hansberry had hoped, so the victory was bittersweet. The Court's ruling facilitated a change in the situation of Carl Hansberry's family, but it did not dramatically affect the lives of other African Americans. However, as Wilkerson demonstrates, Lorraine Hansberry continued this fight for integration during her college years in Wisconsin.

FROM MARGARET B. WILKERSON, "EXCAVATING OUR HISTORY:
THE IMPORTANCE OF BIOGRAPHIES OF WOMEN OF COLOR"
(*Black American Literature Forum*, 1990)

. . . I found that Hansberry came from a very middle-class family whose lifestyle affirmed certain bourgeois values and opportunities—chauffeur, summer vacations, and the like. Most friends and relatives remember her mother not as the fabled Mama of *A Raisin in the Sun*, but rather as the society matron lying on a chaise lounge with a cigarette in a cigarette holder held in her mouth. Lorraine's father, a successful real estate broker, ran for Congress in 1940 on the Republican ticket. Lorraine was one of the lucky and well-off who had a car to drive during her senior year of high school. (77–78)

• • •

. . . I spent two days in the archives of the University of Wisconsin at Madison searching for some evidence of Hansberry's two-year tenure there. My long search through two years of campus newspapers resulted in several articles which mentioned her name as the first black woman to integrate her dormitory *and* a previously unknown letter written by Hansberry to the editor protesting housing discrimination. As important, however, was the fact that these newspapers evoked the Madison campus environment in the late 1940s. The juxtaposition of progressive student activity and traditional fraternity business was stunning! For example, in one January 1948 issue, the front page of the *Daily Cardinal* carried headlines about students organizing to back Wallace, the progressive candidate, and, with equal billing, a story noting that "Opening Sales [in local stores] Hit 1000 as Prom Rush Begins" (23 Jan. 1948). Or an earlier issue that reported on the front page Gandhi's threatening a hunger strike to get warring Indian factions to lay down their arms, alongside an article noting that New York statistics claim Madison to be one of the best spots to latch onto a male—touting the campus as a great one for coeds (13 Jan. 1948). There, running throughout the newspaper, was the specific evidence of trends and movements that we now generalize about. To read it in those papers was to conjure up that world, to step inside its contradictions and to peer out at it through the developing political consciousness of a nineteen-year-old Lorraine. (79)

• • •

. . . Granted her father ran for the Senate on the Republican ticket in 1940 (remember many blacks were Republicans in those days of Southern Dixiecrats), but he also waged a continuous war against racial segregation, carrying a housing discrimination case to the Supreme Court. Unfortunately, he won a narrow ruling, which did not end housing discrimination in Chicago as he had hoped. Disappointed and disillusioned, he exiled himself to Mexico and was preparing to move his family there when he died suddenly.

Lorraine Hansberry, despite her bourgeois upbringing, had seen the fruit of racism and segregation in the struggles of her neighbors who came from all classes, since all blacks were confined to the Black Metropolis, Bronzeville, of Chicago. She had seen the personal toll on her father, and herself had been the near-victim of a mob protesting her family's move into a white neighborhood. . . . Part of Hansberry's achievement in *A Raisin in the Sun* was to embody progressive ideas in the life and struggle of a black family (without resorting to the jargon of the left), and to build that family into a metaphor that whites and blacks, liberals, radicals, and even some conservatives could affirm, *while* winning one of the most prized awards of the theatre establishment. She managed it so well that the two FBI agents who saw the Broadway production and reported on its political import to the Bureau saw no revolutionary danger in the play. They, of course, did not realize that Walter Lee's sons and Mama's daughters would stride the boards in the next two decades, changing for good the image of blacks in the theatre and creating the artistic arm of the black nationalist movement. The line of Hansberry's influence stretches into and beyond the 1960s, but it begins in the 1930s and 1940s as she grew up in the peculiar crucible of segregation known as Chicago. (80–81)

NATHAN HARE

In this article Nathan Hare describes a race riot that occurred in Chicago in 1919. This riot was precipitated by the practice of segregating Lake Michigan, which borders Chicago, as well as the city itself. The drowning of one boy touched off the riot that followed, but as Hare demonstrates, this was not an isolated incident. The tension in Chicago over the issue of race nearly guaranteed that violence would erupt. Rather than simply cite statistics, Hare relies on extended narrative examples to personalize the event so that readers understand it on an emotional as well as an intellectual level. Hare contextualizes this event by relying on the examples of two men—one black and one white—who were both killed during the riot. He presents a "typical" white perspective, Casmere Lazzeroni's, and a "typical" black perspective, James Crawford's, on race relations at the time, and his examples illustrate the probability that many victims of events such as this one were not necessarily directly involved in provoking the violence. By extension, Hare suggests not only that these two men can help us understand the riot of 1919, but also that this riot can help us understand many others. As we know, such violence was not eliminated after 1919. This is a fact that *A Raisin in the Sun* repeatedly raises, from the opening scene when Walter reads about another bombing, through Mrs. Johnson's speculation that the Youngers may themselves be victims of a bombing, to Karl Lindner's warning that other segregationists won't be as reasonable as he claims to be.

FROM NATHAN HARE, "THE DAY THE 'RACE WAR' STRUCK
CHICAGO"
(The Negro History Bulletin, 1962)

In the late afternoon of Sunday, July 27, 1919, a lone Negro boy, 17-year-old Eugene Williams, was swimming offshore in Lake Michigan near 29th Street. The sun was hot (for Chicago even in summer), and the beach sands swarmed with white sun-bathers. Behind Eugene, back to 27th Street, lay a crowd of frolicking Negroes.

Presently, four of the Negro men went over to the "white side" of the beach, walked through the crowd, and entered the water there. They immediately were mobbed by white men and chased out of the water, but returned subsequently with other Negroes to help them. A series of stone-throwing clashes ensued, while women and children scrambled for cover behind rocks and debris.

By now Eugene had drifted beyond the imaginary boundary separating the white and Negro sections of the lake waters. Suddenly, a barrage of stones for which Eugene was the target fell about him, and the boy had to grab a nearby railroad tie and cling to it to stay above water. At this point, a white boy jumped into the water and swam angrily toward him. It was then that Eugene, under pressure of the avalanche of stones, and possibly also through fear and exhaustion, let go of the tie and sank from sight. Now white and Negro men, fearing tragedy, began diving for the boy, over and over, without success. A full hour passed. Still, the boy had not been found.

Meanwhile, a white policeman, Officer Callahan, had arrived at the scene of the commotion. The white officer was importuned by the Negroes present to arrest a white man accused of striking Eugene with a fatal stone. But, over the protests of the Negroes, the white officer refused to arrest the white man. Contrarily, in fact, he arrested a Negro on a white man's complaint.

This unleashed pandemonium, as latent hostility broke out in open battle. Outraged Negroes stormed the white policeman; and one of the most vicious race riots (later to be called Chicago's "race war") was under way. It was to leave 38 persons dead, 537 injured, and approximately 1,000 homeless and destitute. Why did it really happen?

To get an answer, we shall reconstruct, briefly, the day the riot took place, with special reference to the social and racial context leading up to the encounter. We shall not be concerned primarily with the nature of the rioting itself and the characteristics of the rioters. For, the thesis here set forth is not that riots are launched and executed solely by lawless elements and incorrigible mobs. Rather, this case history is employed to demonstrate that riots also involve "normal" individuals and occur when a society or community succumbs to a peculiar condition. It is fitting to choose Chicago's riot of 1919, because, whenever persons familiar with the history of riots in the United States gather to talk about race riots, they, sooner or later, always get around to the Chicago riot of 1919.

Chicago, July 27, 1919

Follow the day of Casmere Lazzeroni, a white man living in Chicago on the morning of July 27, 1919; or, alternately, a Negro resident, James Crawford. Neither, though he had no forewarning, would live through the next forty hours. But, on this, our imaginary daybreak, each begins the routine of his day with perhaps a few of the following concerns then prevalent in Chicago flashing ever so briefly through his consciousness.

Lazzeroni no doubt—assuming he typified the white individuals of his section of the city—felt pangs of anger, even fear, as he walked out into the streets and saw the ghetto of Negro migrants daily overflowing toward his own neighborhood, and who, as impoverished refugees from Southern tenant farms, had more than doubled Chicago's Negro population in the past three years alone. These migrant Negroes were regularly pitted against the white factory workers as strikebreakers, posing thereby a threat to white working class economic potential. Some white individuals also wondered if one or more Negroes were not responsible for the two white girls missing on separate occasions and currently receiving sensational coverage in local white newspapers. Perhaps, too, on this morning, Lazzeroni recalled with scorn how the last of Chicago's World War I Negro soldiers had returned home from Paris the day before; and how the Negro troops had been paraded down Michigan Avenue in the heart of Chicago's Loop, against a background of newspaper reports of their free access in Paris to privileges denied them in the Chicago community.

On the other hand, as James Crawford, the Negro citizen, you now were summarily disillusioned by the North's default in providing the refuge you had hoped for and expected from the racial oppression you had left behind—you thought—in the South. True, it was not then hard, especially, for a Negro to find work in Chicago, but increasingly of late, Negro individuals were being attacked singly and beaten to death by resentful whites.

One young Negro, Charles W. Jackson, had to jump from an elevated right of way of the Chicago, Burlington & Quincy Railroad to Wood and

15th streets, in his effort to flee a white mob. He suffered a broken neck and died instantly. Result: his brother who had come to his rescue, wounding three whites, was the only person arrested. The Jacksons had been living in a neighborhood where the entrance of several Negro families the year before had offended the whites, who circulated a petition asking the Negroes to move out. The Negroes refused to leave.

Two other Negroes had been caught and killed by brutal mobs in weeks past, and others regularly were molested in parks, playgrounds and on beaches. In addition, the mobs were especially prone to bomb the homes of Negroes moving into "white areas." Twenty-four had been the objects of blasts in the past three weeks. You resented the fact, as a Negro, that police were not apprehending and punishing those guilty, even in cases where it seemed easy to do so. And you read with interest, along with your white counterpart, the newspaper accounts of riots taking place in the nation's capital. All of this fanned the half-forgotten flames of recent clashes in East St. Louis, Illinois, and Springfield and other places proximate to Chicago. (123–24)

THEODORE DREISER'S *SISTER CARRIE*

This novel is among Dreiser's most well-known works. In it, Carrie Meeber arrives from a small Wisconsin town to live with her sister and brother-in-law in Chicago at the end of the nineteenth century. Her awe at the city provides Dreiser with an opportunity to describe the incredible growth the city is about to undergo. In the section excerpted here, the narrator presents a Chicago where fortunes could be made, lost, and remade. Although distinctions are not presented in a racial context in this novel, differences between rich and poor, between privileged and disenfranchised, are undeniable. Carrie's brother-in-law might represent the working-class white people whom Nathan Hare describes in the previous excerpt as resenting black members of the community for taking jobs they feel belong to them. At this point Chicago was becoming much more prominent commercially, and its geographic position made it attractive to railroad companies that transported raw materials and manufactured goods, as well as passengers, across the country. Even as this growth energized residents of the city, the scale of development and exchange of large sums of money intimidated newcomers like Carrie. Years later, as these economic divisions remain and become even more clearly affiliated with race, a character such as Walter Younger would also notice them; but rather than be intimidated, he grows resentful and angry. In a sense Carrie's predicament is similar to Walter's, for she needs work, but those with the power to employ her are also powerful enough to refuse to pay her anything above a subsistence wage. Although Carrie notices the evidence of employment, she can barely imagine what actual work gets done—what tasks are performed, what goods produced—and at this point Chicago remains partially a fantasy.

FROM THEODORE DREISER, *SISTER CARRIE*
(Houghton Mifflin, 1969 [orginally published 1900])

In 1889 Chicago had the peculiar qualifications of growth which made such adventuresome pilgrimages even on the part of young girls plausible. Its many and growing commercial opportunities gave it widespread fame, which made of it a giant magnet, drawing to itself, from all quarters, the hopeful and the hopeless—those who had their fortune yet to make and those whose fortunes and affairs had reached a disastrous climax elsewhere. It was a city of over 500,000, with the ambition, the daring, the activity of a metropolis of a million. Its streets and houses were already scattered over an area of seventy-five square miles. Its population was not so much thriving upon established commerce as upon the industries which prepared for the arrival of others. The sound of the hammer engaged upon the erection of new structures was everywhere heard. Great industries were moving in. The huge railroad corporations which had long before recognized the prospects of the place had seized upon vast tracts of land for transfer and shipping purposes. Street-car lines had been extended far out into the open country in anticipation of rapid growth. The city had laid miles and miles of streets and sewers through regions where, perhaps, one solitary house stood out alone—a pioneer of the populous ways to be. There were regions open to the sweeping winds and rain, which were yet lighted throughout the night with long, blinking lines of gas-lamps, fluttering in the wind. Narrow board walks extended out, passing here a house, and there a store, at far intervals, eventually ending on the open prairie.

In the central portion was the vast wholesale and shopping district, to which the uninformed seeker for work usually drifted. It was a characteristic of Chicago then, and one not generally shared by other cities, that individual firms of any pretension occupied individual buildings. The presence of ample ground made this possible. It gave an imposing appearance to most of the wholesale houses, whose offices were upon the ground floor and in plain view of the street. The large plates of window glass, now so common, were then rapidly coming into use, and gave to the ground floor offices a distinguished and prosperous look. The casual wanderer could see as he passed a polished array of office fixtures, much frosted glass, clerks hard at work, and genteel business men in "nobby" suits and clean linen lounging about or sitting in groups. Polished brass or nickel signs at the square stone entrances announced the firm and the nature of the business in rather neat and reserved terms. The entire metropolitan centre possessed a high and mighty air calculated to overawe and abash the common applicant, and to make the gulf between poverty and success seem both wide and deep.

Into this important commercial region the timid Carrie went. She walked east along Van Buren Street through a region of lessening importance, until it deteriorated into a mass of shanties and coal-yards, and finally verged upon the river. She walked bravely forward, led by an honest desire to find employment and delayed at every step by the interest of the unfolding scene, and a sense of helplessness amid so much evidence of power and force which she did not understand. These vast buildings, what were they? These strange energies and huge interests, for what purposes were they there? She could have understood the meaning of a little stone-cutter's yard at Columbia City, carving little pieces of marble for individual use, but when the yards of some huge stone corporation came into view, filled with spur tracks and flat cars, transpierced by docks from the river and traversed overhead by immense trundling cranes of wood and steel, it lost all significance in her little world.

It was so with the vast railroad yards, with the crowded array of vessels she saw at the river, and the huge factories over the way, lining the water's edge. Through the open windows she could see the figures of men and women in working aprons, moving busily about. The great streets were wall-lined mysteries to her; the vast offices, strange mazes which concerned far-off individuals of importance. She could only think of people connected with them as counting money, dressing magnificently, and riding in carriages. What they dealt in, how they laboured, to what end it all came, she had only the vaguest conception. It was all wonderful, all vast, all far removed, and she sank in spirit inwardly and fluttered feebly at the heart as she thought of entering any one of these mighty concerns and asking for something to do—something that she could do—anything. (16–18)

UPTON SINCLAIR'S *THE JUNGLE*

The Jungle was written as an exposé of the meat-packing industry and contains several gruesome scenes describing conditions in the stockyards. When it was initially published, this novel created a scandal regarding the meat-packing business. Consumers were appalled at the conditions in meat-packing plants and at the lack of government regulation of the processing of their food. Although this novel is fiction rather than overt reporting, it had an effect on the reading public that one might more readily expect from investigative journalism.

Earlier in this century, stockyards were a well-known feature of Chicago because of its accessibility by railroad. The city provided a point of transition and transaction between the agricultural West and the populous East. In the section of the novel excerpted here, the stockyards are described in their enormity as well as in their repulsiveness. A group of people are touring the stockyards, and the narrator describes what they see and hear. As well, Sinclair alludes to his theme—that human beings are little different from hogs or cattle as they are herded toward a violent death without time for reflection. Although these workers are not employed directly as servants, they are nevertheless deprived of economic choice; they are no more likely to become the executives making lucrative deals in extravagant restaurants that Walter envies than he is himself. And their work is certainly as distasteful as Mama's when she describes her hands carrying someone else's "slop jars" (103). But perhaps the primary difference between the characters represented here in *The Jungle* and Walter Younger is Walter's determination not to let his present condition become his "destiny."

FROM UPTON SINCLAIR, *THE JUNGLE*
(Airmont, 1965 [orginally published 1906])

They passed down the busy street that led to the yards. It was still early morning, and everything was at its high tide of activity. A steady stream of employees was pouring through the gate—employees of the higher sort, at this hour, clerks and stenographers and such. For the women there were waiting big two-horse wagons, which set off at a gallop as fast as they were filled. In the distance there was heard again the lowing of the cattle, a sound as of a far-off ocean calling. They followed it this time, as eager as children in sight of a circus menagerie—which, indeed, the scene a good deal resembled. They crossed the railroad tracks, and then on each side of the street were the pens full of cattle; they would have stopped to look, but Jokubas hurried them on, to where there was a stairway and a raised gallery, from which everything could be seen. Here they stood, staring, breathless with wonder.

There is over a square mile of space in the yards, and more than half of it is occupied by cattle pens; north and south as far as the eye can reach there stretches a sea of pens. And they were all filled—so many cattle no one had ever dreamed existed in the world. Red cattle, black, white, and yellow cattle; old cattle and young cattle; great bellowing bulls and little calves not an hour born; meek-eyed milch cows and fierce, long-horned Texas steers. The sound of them here was as of all the barnyards of the universe; and as for counting them—it would have taken all day simply to count the pens. . . . (37)

There were two hundred and fifty miles of track within the yards, their guide went on to tell them. They brought about ten thousand head of cattle every day, and as many hogs, and half as many sheep—which meant some eight or ten million live creatures turned into food every year. One stood and watched, and little by little caught the drift of the tide, as it set in the direction of the packing houses. There were groups of cattle being driven to the chutes, which were roadways about fifteen feet wide, raised high above the pens. In these chutes the stream of animals was continuous; it was quite uncanny to watch them, pressing on to their fate, all unsuspicious—a very river of death. Our friends were not poetical, and the sight suggested to them no metaphors of human destiny; they thought only of the wonderful efficiency of it all. The chutes into which the hogs went climbed high up—to the very top of the distant buildings, and Jokubas explained that the hogs went up by the power of their own legs, and then their weight carried them back through all the processes necessary to make them into pork. (38)

• • •

At the same instant the ear was assailed by a most terrifying shriek; the visitors started in alarm, the women turned pale and shrank back. The shriek was followed by another, louder and yet more agonizing—for once started upon that journey, the hog never came back; at the top of the wheel he was shunted off upon a trolley, and went sailing down the room. And meantime another was swung up, and then another and another, until there was a double line of them, each dangling by a foot and kicking in frenzy—and squealing. The uproar was appalling, perilous to the eardrums; one feared there was too much sound for the room to hold—that the walls must give way or the ceiling crack. There were high squeals and low squeals, grunts, and wails of agony; there would come a momentary lull, and then a fresh outburst, louder than ever, surging up to a deafening climax. It was too much for some of the visitors—the men would look at each other, laughing nervously, and the women would stand with hands clenched, and the blood rushing to their faces, and the tears starting in their eyes.

Meantime, heedless of all these things, the men upon the floor were going about their work. Neither squeals of hogs nor tears of visitors made any difference to them; one by one they hooked up the hogs, and one by one with a swift stroke they slit their throats. There was a long line of hogs, with squeals and life-blood ebbing away together, until at last each started again, and vanished with a splash into a huge vat of boiling water. (39–40)

• • •

The carcass hog was scooped out of the vat by machinery, and then it fell to the second floor, passing on the way through a wonderful machine with numerous scrapers, which adjusted themselves to the size and shape of the animal, and sent it out at the other end with nearly all of its bristles removed. It was then again strung up by machinery, and sent upon another trolley ride; this time passing between two lines of men, who sat upon a raised platform, each doing a certain single thing to the carcass as it came to him. One scraped the outside of a leg; another scraped the inside of the same leg. One with a swift stroke cut the throat; another with two swift strokes severed the head, which fell to the floor and vanished through a hole. Another made a slit down the body; a second opened the body wider; a third with a saw cut the breastbone; a fourth loosened the entrails; a fifth pulled them out—and they also slid through a hole in the floor. There were men to scrape each side and men to scrape the back; there were men to clean the carcass inside, to trim it and wash it. Looking down this room, one saw, creeping slowly, a line of dangling hogs a hundred yards in length; and for every yard there was a man, working as if a demon were after him. At the end of this hog's progress every inch of the carcass had been gone over several times, and then it was rolled into the chilling room, where it stayed for twenty-four hours, and where a stranger might lose himself in a forest of freezing hogs. (41)

JANE ADDAMS'S *TWENTY YEARS AT HULL-HOUSE*

Chicago is known for its ethnic neighborhoods, and their establishment paralleled the waves of immigration that occurred in the United States. The newer ethnic groups were discriminated against by those who had been born in the United States and considered themselves "real" Americans, as African Americans were discriminated against after they began to arrive in large numbers in Chicago.

Jane Addams, a social reformer, established a settlement house known as Hull-House on Chicago's north side during the late nineteenth century. (Settlement houses were community service centers established in poor urban areas to provide assistance to people in the neighborhood.) Her book, *Twenty Years at Hull-House*, is as much a social and political document as an autobiography. She discusses her experiences in order to urge social change. In the passage excerpted here, she contextualizes the difficulties of moving from a small European village to a growing and crowded American city. She focuses on the problem of garbage in part because it is local—people in wealthier neighborhoods could hire others to dispose of their garbage for them—and in part because it has so many distasteful connotations. Garbage smells. Garbage draws rats, which breed disease and which themselves have horrifying connotations, as we see in Hansberry's play when Beneatha observes Travis chasing a rat outside their apartment. Jane Addams is equally horrified that children play in this garbage; moreover, children are most likely to evoke her readers' sympathy. (Although Hansberry does not comment specifically on garbage, rats would not have been drawn to the area if there had not been a ready food source.) Thus, the issue of garbage could shock Addams's readers out of their complacency.

FROM JANE ADDAMS, *TWENTY YEARS AT HULL-HOUSE*
(University of Illinois Press, 1990 [originally published 1910])

One of the striking features of our neighborhood twenty years ago, and one to which we never became reconciled, was the presence of huge wooden garbage boxes fastened to the street pavement in which the undisturbed refuse accumulated day by day. The system of garbage collecting was inadequate throughout the city, but it became the greatest menace in a ward such as ours, where the normal amount of waste was much increased by the decayed fruit and vegetables discarded by the Italian and Greek fruit peddlers, and by the residuum left over from the piles of filthy rags which were fished out of the city dumps and brought to the homes of the rag pickers for further sorting and washing.

The children of our neighborhood twenty years ago played their games in and around these huge garbage boxes. They were the first objects that a toddling child learned to climb; their bulk afforded a barricade and their contents provided missiles in all the battles of the older boys; and finally they became the seats upon which absorbed lovers held enchanted converse. We are obliged to remember that all children eat everything which they find and that odors have a curious and intimate power of entwining themselves into our tenderest memories, before even the residents of Hull-House can understand their own early enthusiasm for the removal of these boxes and the establishment of a better system of refuse collection.

It is easy for even the most conscientious citizen of Chicago to forget the foul smells of the stockyards and the garbage dumps, when he is living so far from them that he is only occasionally made conscious of their existence, but the residents of a Settlement are perforce constantly surrounded by them. During our first three years on Halsted Street, we had established a small incinerator at Hull-House and we had many times reported the untoward conditions of the ward to the City Hall. We had also arranged many talks for the immigrants, pointing out that although a woman may sweep her own doorway in her native village and allow the refuse to innocently decay in the open air and sunshine, in a crowded city quarter, if the garbage is not properly collected and destroyed, a tenement-house mother may see her children sicken and die, and that the immigrants must, therefore, not only keep their own houses clean, but must also help the authorities to keep the city clean. (164–65)

CARL SANDBURG'S "CHICAGO"

This well-known and often-quoted poem presents a different attitude toward Chicago from many of the texts excerpted here. Although he also cites the stockyards and railroads and destitute immigrants, Sandburg celebrates the city. Chicago becomes for him a necessary element of America—it works hard; it is masculine. Rather than protest against the difficulties of such a city, Sandburg anticipates the positive results of the inhabitants' arduous lives. Presumably, however, the people most likely to benefit from this work would not be the individuals who actually performed it. On the other hand, in part because he has written a poem rather than a piece of fiction, Sandburg does not develop characters whose lives must be examined more fully. Rather, the people he refers to function as symbols rather than as individuals.

CARL SANDBURG, "CHICAGO"
(1916)

Hog Butcher for the World,
Tool Maker, Stacker of Wheat,

Player with Railroads and the Nation's Freight Handler;
Stormy, husky, brawling,
City of the Big Shoulders:
They tell me you are wicked and I believe them, for I have seen
    your painted women under the gas lamps luring the farm boys.
And they tell me you are crooked and I answer: Yes, it is true I
    have seen the gunman kill and go free again.
And they tell me you are brutal and my reply is: On the faces of
    women and children I have seen the marks of wanton hunger.
And having answered so I turn once more to those who sneer at
    this my city, and I give them back the sneer and say to them:
Come and show me another city with lifted head singing so
    proud to be alive and coarse and strong and cunning.
Flinging magnetic curses amid the toil of piling job on job, here is
    a tall bold slugger set vivid against the little soft cities;
Fierce as a dog with tongue lapping for action, cunning as a
    savage pitted against the wilderness,
Bareheaded,
Shoveling,
Wrecking,
Planning,
Building, breaking, rebuilding,
Under the smoke, dust all over his mouth, laughing with white
    teeth,
Under the terrible burden of destiny laughing as a young man
    laughs,
Laughing even as an ignorant fighter laughs who has never lost a
    battle,
Bragging and laughing that under his wrist is the pulse, and
    under his ribs the heart of the people,
        Laughing!
Laughing the stormy, husky, brawling laughter of Youth, half-
    naked, sweating, proud to be Hog Butcher, Tool Maker, Stacker
    of Wheat, Player with Railroads and Freight Handler to the
    Nation.

RICHARD WRIGHT'S *NATIVE SON*

Of the excerpts presented here, *Native Son* is closest to *A Raisin in the Sun* in terms of thematic concerns. The novel concerns a black family—in particular a black man, Bigger Thomas, and his relationships to his white landlord and employer, as well as to white culture at large. In the scene excerpted here, reminiscent of the moment when Travis is seen by Beneatha as he chases a rat off-stage, Bigger Thomas attempts to kill a rat that has invaded the family's apartment. There is nothing adventuresome about this rat; it is fierce and frightening. The scene is intended to horrify the reader and prompt him or her to judge the responsibility of a landlord who would permit such conditions to exist.

Native Son differs from *A Raisin in the Sun* most dramatically in terms of its tradition. Most critics view *Native Son* as a naturalist novel, whereas *A Raisin in the Sun* falls more within the realist tradition. (Upton Sinclair's *The Jungle*, excerpted above, is also in the naturalist tradition.) In naturalist literature the characters generally are defeated by nature, or the primitive characteristics of society; they cannot hope to escape their destiny. Both naturalism and realism attempt to portray life as it really is rather than to romanticize it, but naturalism is much more pessimistic than realism. Within the tradition of realism, characters can hope to achieve their goals. Although realist literature addresses the difficulties of life, it does not present life as brutally as naturalism does. For our purposes, the easiest way to distinguish the two traditions is with the passage below. Within *A Raisin in the Sun* the incident with the rat is a minor detail that drives home a point. In *Native Son* the incident represents the major issue in the novel.

FROM RICHARD WRIGHT, *NATIVE SON*
(1940)

A huge black rat squealed and leaped at Bigger's trouser-leg and snagged it in his teeth, hanging on.

. . . The force of his movement shook the rat loose and it sailed through the air and struck a wall. Instantly, it rolled over and leaped again. Bigger dodged and the rat landed against a table leg. With clenched teeth, Bigger held the skillet; he was afraid to hurl it, fearing that he might miss. The rat squeaked and turned and ran in a narrow circle, looking for a place to hide; it leaped past Bigger and scurried on dry rasping feet to one side of the box and then to the other, searching for the hold. Then it turned and reared upon its hind legs.

• • •

The rat's belly pulsed with fear. Bigger advanced a step and the rat emitted a long thin song of defiance, its black beady eyes glittering, its tiny forefeet pawing the air restlessly. Bigger swung the skillet; it skidded over the floor, missing the rat, . . .

• • •

Bigger aimed and let the skillet fly with a heavy grunt. There was a shattering of wood as the box caved in. The woman screamed and hid her face in her hands. Bigger tip-toed forward and peered.

"I got 'im," he muttered, his clenched teeth bared in a smile. (9–10)

TOPICS FOR WRITTEN OR ORAL EXPLORATION

1. Examine another play and discuss the significance of the setting as it impacts the characters or the plot. Some suggestions would be *A Streetcar Named Desire* by Tennessee Williams, *Death of a Salesman* by Arthur Miller, or *Trifles* by Susan Glaspell.

2. Write an essay discussing the influence of Chicago on the life of a writer associated with the city. Possibilities include Carl Sandburg, Saul Bellow, Ernest Hemingway, and Gwendolyn Brooks.

3. Research the history of another city or town. Consider how major national events—such as a war, the Depression, or the civil rights movement—affected life in that city or town.

4. Write a poem in which you characterize a place with which you are familiar.

5. Arrange a tour or field trip to an industrial location near where you live or attend school. Write a description of the activity that occurs there.

6. Imagine that you have just arrived in your town after having grown up in an entirely different region. What would strike you as most peculiar or most unusual? Why? Explain your reactions.

7. Discuss the scene in which Walter describes his drives to Indiana and Wisconsin. How do his descriptions of these areas compare or contrast to the way his own neighborhood is described?

8. After reading the selections included in this chapter from *The Jungle* and from *Twenty Years at Hull-House*, discuss whether *A Raisin in the Sun* fits into the tradition of protest literature. If not, what are the characteristics of protest literature that *A Raisin in the Sun* lacks? If so, what is Hansberry attempting to persuade her audience to do?

9. Write an essay discussing the details that make the setting of *A Raisin in the Sun* necessarily urban. Consider, for example, Walter's job, Travis's means of earning money, the proximity of neighbors, etc.

10. Write an essay describing your personal response to the excerpt from either *Sister Carrie, The Jungle*, or *Native Son*. What emotions does the passage evoke from you?

SUGGESTED READINGS

Balter, Alan. *Divided Apple: A Story about Teaching in Chicago*. Dubuque, IA: Kendall-Hunt, 1994.

Chicago Commission on Race Relations. *The Negro in Chicago: A Study of Race Relations and a Race Riot in 1919*. New York: Arno, 1968.

Drake, St. Clair, and Horace R. Cayton. *Black Metropolis: A Study of Negro Life in a Northern City*. Chicago: University of Chicago Press, 1993.

Dybek, Stuart. *The Coast of Chicago*. New York: Random House, 1991.

Grossman, James R. *Land of Hope: Chicago, Black Southerners, and the Great Migration*. Chicago: University of Chicago Press, 1989.

Hansberry, Lorraine. *To Be Young, Gifted, and Black*. New York: Vintage Books, 1995.

Hirsch, Arnold R. *Making the Second Ghetto: Race and Housing in Chicago, 1940–1960*. New York: Cambridge University Press, 1985.

Lowe, David. *The Great Chicago Fire in Eyewitness Accounts and Sixty-Three Contemporary Photographs and Illustrations*. New York: Dover, 1979.

McQuade, Molly. *An Unsentimental Education: Writers and Chicago*. Chicago: University of Chicago Press, 1995.

Pacyga, Dominic A., et al. *Chicago: City of Neighborhoods*. Chicago: Loyola Press, 1986.

Philpott, Thomas L. *The Slum and the Ghetto: Immigrants, Blacks and Reformers in Chicago, 1880–1930*. Belmont, CA: Wadsworth Press, 1991.

Tuttle, William M., Jr. *Race Riot: Chicago in the Red Summer of 1919*. Urbana: University of Illinois Press, 1996.

5

Interpretations of Gender in African American Relationships

Just as *A Raisin in the Sun* addresses many aspects of race relations that would reach crisis points in American culture during the 1960s, it also addresses aspects of gender relations that would emerge with equal urgency during the decades following the play's initial production. As African Americans insisted on equal treatment under the law, women also pressed for an end to discrimination on the basis of sex. The concerns of African Americans and women (and particularly African American women) intersect remarkably and prophetically in this play. This is especially pertinent because modern feminism, the movement that emerged during the 1960s, has frequently been accused of addressing the concerns of white middle-class women only.

The complications of gender emerge along two paths in *A Raisin in the Sun*. First, Walter Younger feels unfulfilled as a man because of his subordinate class status outside his home and because of his frustrating status as a "child" within his home. Second, Beneatha may be thwarted in her professional desires not only because she is black but also because the men with whom she relates, including her brother and her boyfriends, refuse to take her goals seriously.

WALTER'S POSITION AS A MAN

From the opening scene of the play, the audience is aware of Walter's desire to apply his father's life insurance money to the purchase of a liquor store. As the play progresses the connection Walter makes between his job as a chauffeur and his feelings of frustration and inadequacy as a man becomes increasingly evident. Walter's definition of a "real" man apparently includes a particular kind of economic independence. His frustration is made worse because as an African American, the jobs available to him in industry or business are limited to the most menial and subservient. Just as Ruth can never be promoted above her station as another woman's maid, Walter can never be promoted above his station as another man's driver. Not only is wealth forbidden to him, but so are opportunity and dignity. He describes his future as a blank space devoid not only of success but of possibility. If he is to escape the classification of servant, his only option is to buy and manage his own business.

Near the end of Act One, Mama acknowledges Walter's frustration but does not yet understand her potential role in alleviating it. When Walter argues that he is an adult and ought to assume adult responsibilities, Mama re-asserts her own authority as head of the household. For Walter, however, functioning as an adult implies that he will assume the status of head of the household— his gender takes precedence over Mama's age. Because he is male, he cannot simultaneously perceive himself as an adult and as subject to a woman's decisions. (Ruth, by contrast, although despairing at the family's poverty, is apparently able to fulfill her responsibilities within the family while also responding deferentially to Mama.) Walter's desire to be the "head" of his family— that is, to control the events that affect the other members—can be interpreted as a residue of the slave system. Indeed, within slavery a primary difference between free white slave owners and their male slaves was the master's ability to rule his household. The master made decisions for his own family and also for his slaves' families, often disregarding the slaves' familial bonds. At the master's whim, slave parents could be sold apart from each other and from their children. When freedom intersected with masculinity, then, the only apparent way to assert masculinity was to exercise similar authority within one's household. Thus, Walter cannot experience himself as either free or a man as long as he relinquishes authority to Mama. Ironically, the catalyst that finally does encourage Mama to surrender her role is Walter's blatant abandonment of his responsibilities.

Mama begins to realize the depth of Walter's frustration when he fails to object to Ruth's decision to have an abortion. Because abortion at the time of the play's writing was illegal and hence unlicensed and unregulated, Ruth would have been endangering her own life in seeking one. For Mama, the salient characteristic of African Americans is their refusal to accept defeat, their determination to survive even in the face of slavery and slaveholders who sold family members separately, lynching, Jim Crow laws that insisted on segregated public facilities, and abject poverty. For Mama, African Americans are defined by their achievements and their insistence on freedom. When Walter appears to condone the possibility of abortion, she sees him as relinquishing his heritage. He appears to say that the survival of his family no longer matters to him. At this moment Mama considers Walter a traitor to his father. By implication, Mama considers Walter a traitor to his entire race.

This scene convinces Mama that her family will collapse if they don't make dramatic changes. Remembering the dreams she had shared with her husband (i.e., dreams of owning a home with enough room for everyone and space for a garden), Mama purchases the house in Clybourne Park. Although the purchase does fulfill her dream and does bring happiness to Ruth, it only thwarts Walter's dream—for although he might then take a different bus home, he'll still be some other man's driver. The scene ends as Walter accuses Mama of "butchering" his dream, a direct reference to Mama's understanding of abortion as an act that butchers dreams by destroying children.

Oddly, when Walter speaks with George Murchison, he does not attribute masculinity to his black middle-class counterpart. Although Walter imagines white men who make lucrative business deals as his masculine ideal, he describes George's style as "faggoty-looking" (85). To some degree, then, and probably not consciously, "being a man" to Walter implies being white. He criticizes George as a college student, for he believes George's studies aren't practical. Disciplines such as sociology and psychology are too passive from Walter's perspective—to him, acquiring knowledge is not as appealing as giving orders. George will never "run a rubber plantation or a steel mill," professions that not only direct wealth to the owners but also demand the supervision of others (85). Implicitly, Walter defines masculinity not only as asserting authority within his household but also as exploiting workers who are dependent on him.

In the next scene Walter acknowledges that he has not gone to work for three days, risking his job and whatever financial security the family has. Having lost any hope for a different future, Walter appears to have simply given up. He stops struggling to achieve his idea of manhood. But Mama acts decisively. Recognizing that the fulfillment of her own dreams might actually be irrelevant to Walter's needs instead of facilitating them, Mama hands him the money and, with it, her role as head of the household. With this apparent rejuvenation of his dreams, Walter makes an immediate connection to his son, Travis, in stark contrast to his earlier apathy regarding the possible termination of Ruth's pregnancy.

Yet an even more intense and degrading defeat awaits Walter before he can achieve true adult dignity. After he loses the insurance money and the hope that it signifies, he enacts the stereotype of a groveling Negro. He does this without irony and thereby seems dangerously close to accepting the racist stereotype as accurate, to believing that his utter defeat by racism is inevitable. Yet when Karl Lindner reappears, Walter is unable to stoop to this shame of accepting prejudiced treatment while Travis serves as a witness. In other words, despite his sense of defeat, Walter retains his belief in the future. Anticipating that Lindner is going to mistreat him, Walter forces an acknowledgment that they are both men. During his conversation with Lindner, Walter recognizes the connection between his own father and his son as a source of pride. Walter is himself the means by which his father's dignity will be passed to the future. In standing up to Lindner, Walter recreates himself as a man. Although others may continue to treat him disrespectfully, he will not surrender to the humiliation they want to inflict.

Here, finally, at the climax of the play, Mama describes Walter as having "come into his manhood" (151). Although she means in part that he has achieved a sense of himself as an adult, she also is referring to the gendered distinctions among adults. For Walter to be an adult, he must attain respect both within and without his household. He must become the acknowledged head of his family, and he must also interact with other adult males as an equal. Because white men such as his boss have reinforced Walter's dependent status, Karl Lindner (another white man) serves as the catalyst for Walter's emergence into manhood. Only through rejecting the degrading expectations of a white man can Walter become a man.

Moreover, at this point in history a character such as Walter can achieve equality with white men only if he also achieves the same authority within his own family that white men enjoy over the women in their families.

BENEATHA'S POSITION AS A WOMAN

At first Beneatha seems to have higher aspirations than Walter. He longs only to escape a life of servitude, but she aspires to be a doctor. For Walter, selling liquor would be a promotion, whereas for Beneatha, anything less than being able to "make people whole" would be a disappointment (133). Yet Beneatha has not yet had her dreams tested, nor has she ever been responsible for supporting herself or a family. Thus, one could argue that Walter's dreams are realistic whereas Beneatha's are not.

Yet given the evidence of the play, Beneatha will not be able to achieve her dreams without negotiating her gender identity. Although her flippant remark that she might never get married shocks her mother and Ruth, Beneatha's other actions indicate that she is moving toward (or at least desires to move toward) a long-term relationship with a man. Despite her stated boredom with him, she dates George, a young man of middle-class background who Mama and Ruth believe would be a good catch. However, Beneatha and George seem to have little in common, especially in terms of their attitudes toward Africa. When Beneatha cuts her hair, George ridicules her and commands her to change her clothes as if he already holds authority over her. Subsequently he dismisses all African culture as primitive and inelegant.

In the following scene, after another date, George attempts to seduce Beneatha; but she discourages him, preferring to discuss the ideas she has discovered through her studies. Temperamentally George is different from Beneatha; his attitude is much more pragmatic. To him, ideas have no value in themselves; they're just hoops through which one jumps on the way to a degree and, presumably, a job with a good salary. Ideas don't engage him; he seems to dismiss his learning as soon as he receives his grades. But it's not simply George's temperament that is offensive to Beneatha. More significant is his dismissal of her because she is a woman. George urges her to define herself entirely in terms of her appearance; he argues that men are simply not interested in women's thoughts. What men want, according to George, is a sexual relationship with an attractive woman; when they want conversation, they go elsewhere. In this scene George is not a sympathetic character. After George leaves, Beneatha describes him without elaboration to Mama as a "fool." This statement links George to Booker T. Washington, who is also described as a fool a few lines later. Mama supports Beneatha's inclination not to see George any longer, for even if he can offer access to the middle class, Mama has no patience with fools.

In some respects George provides a clear contrast to Asagai. For it is Asagai who has encouraged Beneatha to cut her hair and to celebrate her African ancestry rather than attempt to mimic white fashion and taste. Yet even if Asagai's position regarding the African heritage of African Americans remains more sympathetic, Beneatha nevertheless reaches her conclusions through the instruction of her male companion. Whether she agrees with Asagai or with George, in other words, she does not demonstrate an independent intellect within the play, nor does she refer to any significant female friendship or influence. And there is a relationship among Asagai's exotic status (even if Beneatha warns her family not to treat him as exotic), his intellectual and political opinions, and Beneatha's attraction to him. Although the exact cause is unclear (Is Beneatha physically attracted to him because she is attracted to his ideas? Or does she find his ideas attractive because she first has found him physically attractive?), the two levels of attraction—intellectual and physical—do not function independently of each other.

Although Asagai's language may be more sophisticated and his ideas regarding Africa more informed and progressive than George's, both men's ideas regarding gender coincide remarkably. Although Asagai does arrive bearing gifts, he, too, insults Beneatha's appearance. If George criticizes her after she cuts her hair, Asagai suggests that she is unacceptable until she cuts it; according to Asagai, Beneatha's hair isn't styled but "mutilated" (61). In other words, even though Asagai and George disagree about what is attractive, they both assume that the women they date will make themselves over according to the men's preferences. Of course one could argue that most men and women desire to be attractive to their lovers, but there is no analogous scene in the play in which a woman places similar demands on a man.

More significant, perhaps, is Asagai's opinion regarding the potential diversity of gender relations. When Beneatha suggests that men and women can have feelings for each other that extend beyond sexuality, Asagai disagrees. Beneatha asserts that although sexual expression may form a part of her relationship with a man, the relationship itself has other components. She hopes for an intellectual as well as a sexual companion, a partnership she cannot find with George. But Asagai denies her desire: "For a woman it should be enough" to be a man's sexual partner (63). He places no similar limitations on men. Although he does not overtly state that a woman should prepare to be a wife and mother rather than a doctor, his comment clearly indicates that assumption.

After Walter loses the insurance money and Beneatha has sunk into despair, Asagai reprimands her for illusory thinking, that is, for failing to recognize the difficulty of her situation and rise to its challenge. Although Asagai claims to live out his personal ideals, he refuses to honor Beneatha's. Inviting her to Africa, he relies on a fairy tale about a prince and a maiden; he is, in other words, inclined to reinforce rather than challenge gender stereotypes. When she mentions his proposal to Mama, Beneatha casts it as an opportunity to practice medicine in Africa, an option Asagai has not mentioned. Perhaps Beneatha would still become a doctor if she accompanied Asagai to Nigeria, but nothing in the play indicates that Asagai would support that vision. Perhaps, however, Beneatha will eventually prove strong enough to achieve her dreams without a man's support.

The documents that follow address these issues from a variety of perspectives. In the first article, a literary critic, Steven R. Carter, analyzes the male characters in Hansberry's work. The next several articles address the place of black men within relationships, families, and cultures. First, Stuart A. Queen and Robert W. Habenstein discuss one conventional understanding of the black family as matriarchal. Then bell hooks challenges black men to become more responsible within families without becoming insecure when black women also want to assume broader roles. Next, Donald R. Lewis, in an address to the House of Representatives, enumerates the problems facing black families—particularly black men and boys—and the contributions the government has made to those problems as well as the contributions it can make to their solutions. In the following excerpt, Earl Ofari Hutchinson discusses these problems of the black family as they relate specifically to black fathers. In the last article Audre Lorde confronts the relationships between social pressure and conceptions of women's beauty. Lorde discusses the role of illness in her own life and the contradictions society sees between some forms of illness and femininity.

STEVEN R. CARTER'S ANALYSIS

In this article Steven R. Carter first discusses Hansberry's ability to create credible male characters. Readers and critics sometimes assume that writers cannot create characters with whom they do not share identifying characteristics, especially gender and race. Some critics argue that it is easier for an author who is marginalized by virtue of race or gender to create a dominant figure than vice versa; that is, it is easier for a female writer to create a male character than the other way around, because oppressed people must understand their oppressors in order to survive, whereas the opposite is not true. Nevertheless, Carter's argument is accurate; whether or not we find the male characters in this play sympathetic, most readers do find them realistic.

The second section of this excerpt looks specifically at the characters George and Asagai. Carter suggests that Asagai is a more complex character and hence displays more potential for growth than does George. In other words, although Asagai has not yet explored his assumptions regarding gender, his ability to analyze oppressive relationships in other contexts suggests that he may one day also apply his insights to issues of gender.

FROM STEVEN R. CARTER, "IMAGES OF MEN IN LORRAINE
HANSBERRY'S WRITING"
(*Black American Literature Forum*, 1985)

Partially as a result of her belief that ideologies and systems were the true
enemies, she [Hansberry] was able to create many convincing and sympathetic male characters with whom a man could easily identify. At the
same time, she carefully emphasized the ways in which these sympathetic
creations are caught in the web of sympathetic conditioning in male su-
premacy and the resulting harm that they do to women and themselves.
Thus, among her most important male characters are multidimensional
figures who are admirable in many respects, who struggle valiantly
against a variety of personal and social pressures, who frequently arouse
the audience to cheer on their efforts, and who, nevertheless, sometimes
callously and sometimes subtly, oppress the women entangled in their
lives. (160–61)

• • •

In the same play *[A Raisin in the Sun]*, there are two other examples of
male chauvinism. Both of the men interested in Walter Lee's sister, Beneatha, display traditional attitudes toward women, though in varying de-
grees. The middle-class American black George Murchison regards
Beneatha's desire to be a doctor as laughable, and when she tries to talk to
him seriously, he advises her "to cut it out." . . . Not surprisingly, she dismisses him as a fool. Her other suitor, the African student Joseph Asagai,
cannot be so easily dismissed, however, since he is somewhat complex and
appealing. His beguiling mixture of idealism and sophistication, his seem-
ing role as spokesman for many of Hansberry's political and philosophical
views, and his willingness to die either to free his country from colonialism
or simply to aid its progress—all lend him the aura of a romantic hero. . . .
In spite of all his revolutionary attitudes, Asagai is, in this one area, a traditional—and fallible—male. Unlike George Murchison, however, he is
willing to listen to Beneatha and to take her career goals seriously, thus en-
abling their relationship to grow and leaving open the possibility that he
may eventually free himself of his remaining chauvinism. (161)

STUART A. QUEEN AND ROBERT W. HABENSTEIN'S
DESCRIPTION OF THE MATRIARCHAL FAMILY

In this excerpt, published approximately a decade after *A Raisin
in the Sun* was initially performed, Queen and Habenstein describe

a matriarchal version of the Negro family (i.e., led by a woman, generally the mother or grandmother). This view of African American families was commonly held during the 1950s, though it has been challenged more recently by African Americans. The authors posit three categories of the matriarchal family. According to the authors, the Younger family early in the play would fall into the third category, wherein a father is present but does not serve as head of the household. This shifts by the end of the play, when the Younger family can no longer be described as matriarchal.

FROM STUART A. QUEEN AND ROBERT W. HABENSTEIN, *THE
FAMILY IN VARIOUS CULTURES*
(Lippincott, 1967)

In the matriarchal family the mother, or perhaps the maternal grand-mother and daughter, holds dominant influence of property, authority, and household affairs. [Andrew and Amy Tate Billingsley] have distinguished three subtypes of the matriarchal family pattern: (1) father absent, (2) a father or series of fathers temporarily present, and (3) father constantly present. In the last case although the father is present, he usually cannot be the breadwinner or assert parental authority because of his precarious status in the labor market. All three of these sub-types find their roots in traditional Negro family organization. We have noted that by virtue of his occupational status and restricted personal freedom, the slave husband was at best a sometime husband. After emancipation the achievement of a strong parental role was extremely limited if not blocked by his inability to maintain the status of breadwinner for the family. With her acceptance of the dominant role in the family, the Negro female in the mother-centered family came to develop a . . . grim realization that males could not always be trusted to accept normal parental responsibilities. These handicaps are also the legacy of slavery and its aftermath. (319)

BELL HOOKS

bell hooks, the pseudonym of Gloria Watkins, is a prominent cultural critic who has published several books on race relations and African American culture. In the passage excerpted here, hooks first questions why "popular culture" attributes the greatest degree of sexism and sexual violence to black men—why, that is, white culture exploits black culture in order to analyze gender inequities. Yet hooks does acknowledge the tensions that exist between black men and black women. She argues that sexism hurts not only women but also men. Specifically in regard to black culture, she suggests that sexism is a means by which black people are separated from each other—that sexism, in other words, dilutes black cultural and political power. Although the statement she refers to by Malcolm X is often interpreted to condone violence, she suggests that feminism may be one of the "means necessary" for African Americans to achieve complete access to the illusory American dream.

FROM BELL HOOKS, *BLACK LOOKS: RACE AND REPRESENTATION*
(South End Press, 1992)

Most black men remain in a state of denial, refusing to acknowledge the pain in their lives that is caused by sexist thinking and patriarchal, phallocentric violence that is not only expressed by male domination over women but also by internecine conflict among black men. Black people must question why it is that, as white culture has responded to changing gender roles and feminist movement, they have turned to black culture and particularly to black men for articulations of misogyny, sexism, and phallocentrism. In popular culture, representations of black masculinity equate it with brute phallocentrism, woman-hating, a pugilistic "rapist" sexuality, and flagrant disregard for individual rights. (102)

• • •

Solidarity between black women and men continues to be undermined by sexism and misogyny. As black women increasingly oppose and challenge male domination, internecine tensions abound. Publicly, many of the gender conflicts between black women and men have been exposed in recent years with the increasingly successful commodification of black women's writing. Indeed, gender conflict between sexist black male writers and those black female writers who are seen as feminists has been particularly brutal. (107–8)

• • •

Most black men will acknowledge that black men are in crisis and are suffering. Yet they remain reluctant to engage those progressive movements that might serve as meaningful critical interventions, that might allow them to speak their pain. On the terms set by white supremacist patriarchy, black men can name their pain only by talking about themselves in crude ways that reinscribe them in a context of primitivism. Why should black men have to talk about themselves as an "endangered species" in order to gain public recognition of their plight? (112)

• • •

Changing representations of black men must be a collective task. Black people committed to renewed black liberation struggle, the de-colonization of black minds, are fully aware that we must oppose male domination and work to eradicate sexism. There are black women and men who are working together to strengthen our solidarity. . . . If black men and women take seriously Malcolm's charge that we must work for our liberation "by any means necessary," then we must be willing to explore the way feminism as a critique of sexism, as a movement to end sexism and sexist oppression, could aid our struggle to be self-determining. Collectively we can break the life-threatening choke-hold patriarchal masculinity imposes on black men and create life-sustaining visions of a reconstructed black masculinity that can provide black men ways to save their lives and the lives of their brothers and sisters in struggle. (113)

DONALD R. LEWIS

A congressional hearing was held in 1989 to examine problems specific to black male teenagers and young adults. Donald R. Lewis was one of several speakers before the committee. In his address he identifies the family, along with the church, as one of the most effective social structures for instilling a sense of individual responsibility. He suggests that the most effective families are those headed by men, and that it is when men abandon their responsibilities that families suffer. He attributes much of the disruption experienced by black families to interference, intentional or not, with families by the civil government. Some government policies that are intended to assist families and/or children have the long-term effect of destroying those families, he maintains. Lewis urges the House of Representatives to examine potential legislation more seriously so that laws that facilitate short-term progress do not also create long-term harm.

FROM "BARRIERS AND OPPORTUNITIES FOR AMERICA'S YOUNG
BLACK MEN"
Statement of Donald R. Lewis, Director, Nehemiah Project,
Annandale, VA, *Hearing Before the Select Committee on Children,
Youth, and Families, House of Representatives*, 101st Congress,
First Session, July 25, 1989

I am the Director of the Nehemiah project, a counseling and seminar-based effort involving helping black men back to their responsibilities as husbands, fathers, and responsible community leaders.

• • •

. . . [H]istorically, family government has encouraged, if not forced, its members to come to grips with issues such as selfishness, coping with disappointment, personal responsibility, sharing, aggression, forgiveness, as well as forcing its members to develop learning skills, marketable trade skills. Family government has taught children the art of sacrificing personal interests for the family purpose. Personal gratification boundaries were clearly defined by parental authority. Strong—and male-directed—family government produced clear personal government. As a child myself, I knew that if I did not exercise "responsible government" of my personal behavior, the next level of government would take over. That reality molded clear personal identity, security, confidence, and personal discipline.

Historically, for many (especially in the black community) the church has also represented a distinct level of "government." For generations, the black church provided a disenfranchised people with their only opportunity to exercise self government. It gave a sphere of influence that was not allowed in any other arena. Therefore, the black church became the center for social and political activities, resolving intra-community conflicts, and finding mates. Surrounded by moral, ethical, and spiritual standards and generally responsible adults who loved the children, kids soon learned that the local church took their well-being and behavior very seriously. "Church discipline" always supported and reinforced family government.

The institutions of church and family have served us well in the black community. In addition to their other purposes, church and family have represented character formation and behavioral constraint which formed personal disciplines. I must say to the distinguished members of this committee, civil government cannot replace and it must not weaken the church, the family or any other valid governing institution. The cost for such intrusion and presumption is too great.

Nowhere is the cost heavier than on America's young black men. Public policy has, for decades, been undermining and eroding the black family in general and fatherhood in specific. Public policy, in attempting to provide assistance for the deprived, has inadvertently encouraged others into the same patterns of deprivation. Too often, government assistance has financially penalized men who want to be married to the mother of their children. Through decades of social policy . . . the federal government has gutted and plundered the black community of its husbands and fathers.

The result is that boys learn that drugs and larceny are the fastest ways of making lots of cash. They simply don't have fathers who can teach and demonstrate the virtues of a healthy work ethic, the importance of sexual discipline and responsibility, the benefits of education, and the beauty of transcendent values. Therefore, they take their cues from other male influences—pimps, pushers, and thieves—in the community who seem to be "making it." Lacking a father's voice affirming identity, they also turn to street sex for a validation of their manhood.

The institutions of family and church have been the mainstay of a people that couldn't be destroyed by slavery, economic deprivation and other forms of racism. The undermining of those two basic governing influences has opened the door to drugs, crime, sexual promiscuity, unwanted children and the pervasive despair that has emasculated far too many of our young black men.

• • •

. . . [T]oday I call on the federal government to let the wonderful economy, efficiency, and effectiveness of our free society supply missing dimensions of government which will "save the boys." Let men, especially black men, know they are essential to a well ordered, healthy society. Let them know it "rests on their shoulders." They will rise to the challenge. I repeat, they will rise to the challenge.

• • •

We must also learn to analyze and measure public policy by its impact on the family. Government must ask if specific policy proposals weaken or reinforce the stability and cohesion of the home, and in particular the black home. Policymakers must give serious scrutiny to the issue of how government can accord greater respect to the rights of parental government. (112–14)

EARL OFARI HUTCHINSON ON FATHERHOOD

In this excerpt Earl Ofari Hutchinson, an African American author writing primarily to other African Americans, acknowledges that fatherhood for a black man (and to some degree for all men) is more challenging today than ever. Although old problems such as poverty persist, new ones have also arisen. Children are tempted toward drugs, gangs, and violence as never before. And the consequences have grown more serious. Since guns have become so available, for instance, a child who might once have risked injury now risks death. Since the AIDS epidemic has emerged, people who engage in unprotected sex or use intravenous drugs risk their lives with each encounter. Hutchinson also addresses the necessity for black men and black women to overcome their suspicion of each other. Although his tone is not as urgent as bell hooks's is, he seems to agree with her that African American culture cannot easily survive if men and women remain divided.

FROM EARL OFARI HUTCHINSON, *BLACK FATHERHOOD: THE GUIDE TO MALE PARENTING*
(Middle Passage Press, 1995)

While times have changed, black fathers are still handling problems their way. Some of those problems haven't changed. Many African-Americans still face bitter discrimination, poverty and family hardship. Now add to this the tough hurdles of: AIDS, drug addiction, alcoholism, gangs, promiscuous sex and violence, and indeed life can seem like an endless procession of complex and dizzying conflicts and problems.

There is another challenge, perhaps even more perplexing to black men. They must also find a way to break down the barriers of suspicion and distrust between them and their women. Most African-Americans have heard the accusations.

Many black women say black men are: unfaithful, insensitive, exploitive, greedy, selfish and egotistical. In turn, black men say black women are: unfaithful, insensitive, exploitive, greedy, selfish and egotistical. Male-female relationships, including marriage, are an emotional minefield that black fathers must tip lightly through. (14)

AUDRE LORDE AND WOMEN'S IMAGE

Audre Lorde, a black poet who addressed both racism and sexism, battled breast cancer for many years before she died in 1992. In the selection excerpted here from her book examining her experience with cancer, she addresses the ramifications of her illness on her ability to be perceived as a proper woman. Although one could argue that in Hansberry's play the effects on Beneatha Younger when she decides to cut her hair are comparatively innocuous, Lorde argues here that mainstream culture obsesses over a woman's appearance even during life-and-death moments. Lorde points out that a woman herself is pressured to make choices based on the preferences of others—generally, but not always, men. Beneatha's hair was considered attractive or not depending on the preference of the person who observed her; she herself didn't express an opinion outside of that context. Lorde, on the other hand, recognizes the conflict between what feels physically and psychologically comfortable to her and what is acceptable to most people around her. Because Lorde dares to acknowledge this conflict, those people view her as "bizarre."

FROM AUDRE LORDE, *THE CANCER JOURNALS*
(Aunt Lute Books, 1980)

Attitudes toward the necessity for prostheses after breast surgery are merely a reflection of those attitudes within our society towards women in general as objectified and depersonalized sexual conveniences. Women have been programmed to view our bodies only in terms of how they look and feel to others, rather than how they feel to ourselves, and how we wish to use them. We are surrounded by media images portraying women as essentially decorative machines of consumer function, constantly doing battle with rampant decay. (Take your vitamins every day and he *might* keep you, if you don't forget to whiten your teeth, cover up your smells, color your grey hair and iron out your wrinkles. . . .) As women, we fight this depersonalization every day, this pressure toward the conversion of one's own self-image into a media expectation of what might satisfy male demand. The insistence upon breast prostheses as "decent" rather than functional is an additional example of that wipe-out of self in which women are constantly encouraged to take part. I am personally affronted by the message that I am only acceptable if I look "right" or "normal," where those norms have nothing to do with my own perceptions of who I am. Where "normal" means the "right" color, shape, size, or number of breasts, a woman's perception of her own body and the strengths that come from that perception are discouraged, trivialized, and ignored. When I mourn my right breast, it is not the appearance of it I mourn, but the feeling and the fact. But where the superficial is supreme, the idea that a woman can be beautiful and one-breasted is considered depraved, or at best, bizarre, a threat to "morale." (64–65)

TOPICS FOR WRITTEN OR ORAL EXPLORATION

1. The Younger household consists of an extended family of three generations living together. Discuss the function of a family, analyzing the advantages or disadvantages of living within an extended family.

2. At the time this play was originally produced, abortion was illegal in the United States. Discuss Ruth's motivation for seeking an abortion. Does she confirm or contradict your own stereotypes of women who seek abortions?

3. Compare (1) Walter's response to the possibility that Ruth is considering an abortion with (2) Mama's description of her husband's response to the death of their son Claude. What factors do you believe would cause the men to respond the way they do? Do you agree with Mama that Walter is a disgrace because of his response?

4. Compare (1) Mama's response to George Murchison, with (2) Walter's response. How does each one feel about George's access to wealth? How does each one feel about George's masculinity? What do they each believe they have in common with George?

5. George calls Walter a "Prometheus." Research the story of Prometheus and discuss whether you think Walter fits this characterization.

6. Beneatha shocks her family by suggesting she might not get married. Based on evidence in the play, do you believe she will? Explain your answer.

7. Beneatha's desire to be a doctor is unusual for her time because she's both black and a woman. Look up statistics on current gender breakdowns of particular professions (e.g., medicine, law, engineering, education). What do you think are the reasons why some professions remain predominantly male and others predominantly female, while others have become more balanced in their gender makeup?

8. Beneatha says George laughs at her for wanting to be a doctor. Would Asagai? Why or why not?

9. In the original production of this play, the scene in which Beneatha cuts her hair was eliminated. Discuss the possible thematic effects of this decision.

10. Do you agree that Beneatha "mutilates" her hair by straightening it? What other activities could be considered "mutilation"? Discuss such things as make-up, piercing, tattoos, and the like in this context.

11. Beneatha and Asagai disagree about the feelings that exist between men and women. Discuss the extent to which you think all relationships between men and women are founded on romance or sexuality.

12. Why is it important for Walter to replace Mama as the head of the family?

13. Discuss why poverty seems to dehumanize Walter differently than it does the women in the play.

14. Walter links class and sexuality when he ridicules George. Discuss current stereotypes that also link class with sexuality. Consider working-class as well as upper-class stereotypes.

15. Define "being a man" according to Walter, Mama, and Asagai.

16. Compare Walter to prominent male characters in other plays you've read. Examples include Willy Loman in *The Death of a Salesman*, Eugene O'Neill's *Long Day's Journey into Night*, Tennessee Williams's *The Glass Menagerie*, and Edward Albee's *Who's Afraid of Virginia Woolf?*

17. Write a response to Steven R. Carter's analysis of the male characters in *A Raisin in the Sun*. Do you find Carter's argument persuasive and accurate? Agree or disagree, citing specific scenes from the play.

18. After reading the excerpts by hooks, Lewis, and Hutchinson, write a summary of the ways in which African American men are in crisis. You may also refer to current events to expand on your answer or to disagree with these writers.

SUGGESTED READINGS

Berrian, Brenda F. "The Afro-American–West African Marriage Question: Its Literary and Historical Contexts." *African Literature Today* 15 (1987): 152–59.

Cleaver, L. Eldridge. "As Crinkly as Yours." *Negro History Bulletin* (March 1962): 127–32.

Giddings, Paula. *When and Where I Enter: The Impact of Black Women on Race and Sex in America*. New York: William Morrow, 1984.

Hull, Gloria T., Patricia Bell Scott, and Barbara Smith, eds. *All the Women Are White, All the Blacks Are Men, But Some of Us Are Brave: Black Women's Studies*. New York: Feminist Press, 1981.

Omolade, Barbara. *The Rising Song of African American Women*. New York: Routledge, 1990.

Rooks, Noliwe M. *Hair Raising: Beauty, Culture and African American Women*. New Brunswick, NJ: Rutgers University Press, 1996.

Staples, Robert. "The Myth of Black Macho: A Response to Angry Black Feminists." *Black Scholar* (March/April 1979): 24–33.

Walker, Alice. "Beauty: When the Other Dancer Is the Self." In *In Search of Our Mother's Gardens*. New York: Harcourt Brace Jovanovich, 1983, 384–93.

Wallace, Michele. *Invisibility Blues: From Pop to Theory*. New York: Verso, 1990.

Wiegman, Robyn. *American Anatomies: Theorizing Race and Gender*. Durham, NC: Duke University Press, 1995.

6

Contemporary Race Relations

Although two generations have passed since *A Raisin in the Sun* was originally performed, it remains remarkably contemporary. Readers often forget that it was written before the civil rights movement reached its peak in the 1960s. This fact is a credit to Hansberry's writing skill: while writing about the experiences of one particular family, she is nevertheless able to evoke an empathic response from a multitude of readers or viewers who may or may not share characteristics or experiences with the Youngers. (When the play opened on Broadway in 1959, for example, very few members of the audience would have been African American.) And Hansberry is unequivocally a good writer—without being didactic, she effectively conveys a family's history and hopes, conflicts and concord, in slightly more than one hundred pages.

A more pessimistic interpretation of the play's contemporary application is that little has changed in America. Although it is no longer legal, housing segregation is still practiced in many cities and regions. And segregation in housing affects the possibility of integration elsewhere, especially in the schools. The majority of businesses, especially large ones, are owned by white men; and African American students are still underrepresented in many academic disciplines. Most people cannot get through a day without being made aware of racial issues. Even Americans who interact almost exclusively with people of their own racial or ethnic backgrounds read newspapers and watch television programs that discuss issues such as affirmative action and report on crimes that have (or are interpreted to have) a racial component.

Race is likely to remain an area of conflict or tension for several more generations. Indeed, Jim Crow laws existed for generations following the abolition of slavery, and social pressure often functioned to maintain a degree of segregation in places and at times when such laws did not apply. Even today, although many people interact professionally with persons of different races, most Americans socialize primarily with members of their own race. Some people may argue that this country has been built on racial division, that racism is part of the American identity, and that dismantling racism necessitates reconfiguring assumptions about American identity. Yet many contemporary Americans support diversity as a value in and of itself, and most Americans currently support the idea of equality even though they disagree over how to achieve it.

Although the issues raised in *A Raisin in the Sun* remain current, the racial climate in the United States has changed considerably since the 1950s. It is true that many African American children continue to live in poverty and that children living in urban environments today could likely chase a rat for entertainment as Travis does in the play, but it is also true that many other children do live in integrated urban and suburban neighborhoods—many more so than did during the 1950s. Moreover, although African American men in the 1990s suffer from a discouragingly high level of unemployment, Walter Younger's choices today would extend beyond working as a chauffeur or owning a liquor store. And Beneatha would be much more likely to fulfill her dream of being a doctor today than she would have at the time the play was first produced. Recognizing the progress that has been made during the second half of the twentieth century makes it possible to hope for continued progress in the twenty-first century. Even though cultural changes cannot be measured on a day-to-day basis, changes that accrue over decades must be pursued daily.

In a sense, Hansberry's play concludes in an open-ended fashion. The Youngers have decided to risk moving to Clybourne Park, a risk they have been warned against by both a white resident of that neighborhood and a black neighbor in their current neighborhood. Although the play implies that the adjustment will be difficult despite the Youngers' new coherence as a family, as an audience we don't know how they will be treated after the move. Perhaps they will encounter violence, a possibility the play acknowledges. Perhaps they will experience subtler acts of racism. If events of the second half of the twentieth century are any indication of the Youngers' future, their choices for justice will be challenging but not futile.

The documents that follow address several issues that are raised in *A Raisin in the Sun* and explored in this book. The documents in this chapter differ from those in earlier chapters in that they assume the perspective of the late twentieth century. They provide insight into how much circumstances have changed—and how much they have remained the same. First, two recent government documents examine the persistence of discrimination. The first considers the issue in general; the second specifically examines minority-owned businesses. The next two documents examine a particular event—the O.J. Simpson trial—that became a national obsession and was publicly represented and interpreted primarily in terms of the racial identifications of the defendant, the victims, and the members of the jury. On the most immediate level, this case demonstrates the amount of tension that still exists in the United States around the issue of race. In addition, since Simpson is African American and his alleged victims, including the woman to whom he had been married, were white, this event illustrates the anxiety that Ruth refers to in *A Raisin in the Sun* when she says that white people are afraid of interracial marriages. The third set of documents addresses the issue of race and alcohol. In light of Walter Younger's aspirations to own a liquor store, these excerpts analyze the role of alcohol in African American culture as well as in mainstream media. Finally, the last set of documents analyzes the situation of African American children and young adults in terms of education. These documents examine the ways in which the teaching strategies of American public education sometimes are founded on (unintentionally) racist assumptions. These assumptions can range from thoughts about the natural abilities of particular groups of people to their interests, learning styles, and life goals. The excerpts also reveal more personal and individual experiences in the contemporary classroom.

FINDINGS OF THE NATIONAL COMMISSION FOR
EMPLOYMENT POLICY

This 1991 study examines the presence and effect of discrimination in the workplace. It seeks to measure how much progress has been made in the decades since laws forbidding discrimination were passed. Although most social scientists acknowledge that discrimination remains a factor in the American economy, they also acknowledge that such a force is difficult to measure. For example, if a black lawyer and a white lawyer are paid different salaries, how much of that difference can be attributed to discrimination? Social scientists attempt to measure the difference by comparing, for example, people with comparable education and experience. If both lawyers attended the same law school, graduated in the same year, and attained similar class rankings, but were nevertheless offered different salaries, at least some of that difference could be attributed to discrimination. Such comparisons are not always easy to make, however, in part because of minority underrepresentation in various professions and educational institutions. In addition, few employers would acknowledge or even believe that they hired the white man for the job because he was white.

This study also addresses the fact that for women there is a smaller income gap between races. Nevertheless, black families on average remain poorer than white families despite the similar earnings of white and black mothers. This difference is attributed to the distinctions between black and white family structures (black families are more likely to be headed by a single woman) and to the gap between the earnings of the black men and the white men who function as the fathers in these families.

FROM THE NATIONAL COMMISSION FOR EMPLOYMENT
POLICY, *A CHANGING NATION—ITS CHANGING LABOR FORCE*
Research Report #91–04, November 1991

"Discrimination"

Discrimination is recognized as having an important impact on labor market outcomes for minorities and women. However, economists and other social scientists have had great difficulty assessing precisely its impact on earnings and employment. One economic theory assumes that some employers, workers, and unions have a "taste" for discrimination. If this theory is correct, discrimination would diminish over time as nondiscriminatory employers compete successfully in the labor market against those who discriminate.

There have been many efforts to estimate empirically the impact of race/ethnic and sex discrimination, but there is no consensus on how large the effects are. Unlike many economic phenomena, the effects of discrimination must be estimated indirectly. Analysts estimate discrimination statistically through a process of elimination. Various factors such as education, English language proficiency, and other forms of human capital are first examined. When groups are equal, or roughly so, and a disparity remains either in the kind of job offered or in wages paid for similar jobs, this disparity is attributed to "discrimination." The problem with this approach is that one rarely if ever can control for all the relevant factors that determine earnings. Thus, the range of estimated discrimination impacts is quite large. A recent survey of the literature found that black males may earn between 10 and 40% less than white males because of discrimination.

The U.S. Commission on Civil Rights examined the economic and employment status of black women as compared with white women over the period since 1940. It concluded that the gap between black women and white women has largely been closed in terms of earnings and occupational distribution. The report did not address the question of the income gap between men and women.

Despite the improvement in the labor market status of black women workers, they—and their families—have not achieved economic (or social) parity with white women. This is attributed largely to the lower status and earning power of black men. Black women workers frequently either are not married and are raising children alone on a single income or are married to men who earn less and have less economic stability than they (the women) do. (38–39)

FINDINGS OF THE UNITED STATES COMMISSION ON MINORITY BUSINESS DEVELOPMENT

This 1993 study analyzes the growth in minority-owned businesses and the role of those businesses in the American economy. Although the raw numbers may seem to indicate that minority group members contribute a significant amount to the national economy, when those numbers are converted into percentages of the economy it is evident that minorities continue to be underrepresented. Additionally, if "minority-owned" businesses are broken down according to ethnicity, it is clear that businesses owned specifically by African Americans are growing at the slowest rate. The study speculates about the factors reflected in that statistic.

This study also takes a stand on the need for minority-owned businesses in the overall economy. It shifts this discussion from the realm of social work to the discipline of economics. Just as a middle-class economy (in which most citizens would be middle class rather than having extreme gaps between upper and lower class people) depends on a generally well-educated work force, for example, a strong economy depends on the contributions of all citizens. When a society is structured such that roughly 20 percent of its members are excluded from full participation, the economy in general will suffer. The subtext of this assertion is that although white people in the United States are generally better off financially than black people, no group is as financially secure as they might be if the economy were to take advantage of the talents of all citizens.

FROM THE UNITED STATES COMMISSION ON MINORITY
BUSINESS DEVELOPMENT, *FINAL REPORT*
Government Document 43.2: m 66/H62 (1993)

The first Survey of Minority Owned Business Enterprises was conducted in 1969. These studies are undertaken once during each five-year period and the Commission has obtained and reviewed the latest such census which is based on 1987 data. Unfortunately, these data present compelling evidence that minority business is, in fact, a severely underutilized national resource.

The number of minority owned firms grew from 741,640 in 1982 to 1,213,750 in 1987. This is an increase of nearly 65 percent, but minority businesses still account for less than 9 percent of the total of all United States firms. Most of the increase in the number of minority firms came from business growth among Asian and Pacific Islanders (an increase of 167,640 firms over 1982 levels, for a percentage gain of 89.3 percent) and from the Hispanic community (an increase of 188,398 establishments over the same five-year period, for a total gain of 80.5 percent).

In fact, nearly 76 percent of the growth of all minority firms between 1982 and 1987 is attributable to the growth of Asian Pacific and Hispanic owned firms. Given continuation of the present trend, it appears that firms owned by Black Americans (estimated at 424,165 establishments in 1987, evidencing a growth rate of less than 38 percent for the five-year period) will be soon displaced in their first place position, as to numbers of minority firms, by both Hispanics (422,373 establishments in 1987) and Asian-owned firms (355,331 firms in 1987).

The 1.2 million minority owned firms in 1987 had gross receipts of $77.84 billion. This represents an increase of $43.4 billion over the 1982–1987 period. Yet, all firms in the United States had gross receipts of $1.99 trillion in 1987 and, therefore, minority firms were only permitted to contribute a mere 3.9 percent to the National total. (2–3)

• • •

The Commission has compared statistics by major industry category and has found a pattern of disparity across all lines of business endeavor that we believe is correlated to the ethnicity of the business owner. In 1987 the typical minority owned firm's total annual receipts were only 44 percent of the average receipts of all United States firms. In Agriculture/Mining that difference was 51 percent; in Construction 45 percent; in Manufacturing 25 percent; Transportation 37 percent; Wholesale 44 percent; Retail 49 percent; Finance/Insurance–Real Estate 36 percent; and in the Services Industry—where the greatest numerical share of all businesses are located—the typical minority firm had receipts that were only 43 percent of the average service firm in the country. (4)

• • •

We do not have the resources nor the mission to study every aspect of the social, political, and economic systems that have relegated minority owned firms to less than 4 percent of the business activity in this country. The Commission does find, however, that stereotypical images of minority owned firms limit their access to the factors of production. As a result such firms are either directed toward those industries with the lowest capital entrance barriers and, consequently, the most establishments, highest competition, and the highest failure rates; or are made to enter other, less traditional business areas with lower than needed levels of capital and access to financing.

In that latter event, the margin for error in business judgment becomes negligible, thereby reducing the probability for success. In either case, however, our nation's history has created a "cycle of negativity" that reinforces prejudice through its very practice: restraints on capital availability lead to failures and failures, in turn, reinforce a prejudicial perception of minority firms as inherently high-risks, thereby reducing access to even more capital and further increasing the risk of failure. And so the cycle continues. But, the correlation between success and failure is not one based on race, it is one based on the availability of capital—and on its historic allocation.

The Commission is convinced, however, that breaking this cycle will channel talents, creativity, resourcefulness, and entrepreneurial energies into our economic system in a manner that will yield a significant return on investment for all Americans. Succinctly stated, the problem of the underutilization of minority business is not a minority problem. It is an economic problem. It is a problem we all share as Americans. (6)

• • •

Minority business development efforts are not social programs; they are investments in America's economic system and in its future. Even if we place considerations of equity and historic discrimination aside, it makes absolutely no economic sense to squander more than 20 percent of the nation's most precious resource—human talent—and foster, in effect, practices that primarily force minorities to be consumers rather than producers of wealth.

The continued failure of the nation to address directly the problem of underutilization of the talents and creativity of the minority community will escalate in magnitude and become an increasing drain on the nation's wealth. Demands for governmental subsistence programs can only increase to support minimum life sustaining benefits for a permanent underclass that grows larger with each passing year. Such divisiveness presents a prospective danger to both social and economic stability. The Commission urges that the nation invest in human capital now so that it may reap the benefits of economic progress in the future.

The Commission believes that it is the primary responsibility of the Administration and of the Congress to stop presenting minority business programs as special interest programs and to counter often heard allegations that such programs are mere subsidies. The compelling national interest presented by this issue is economic development and how increasing the access of minority group members to the factors of production will generate business activity and contribute to that development. Public persuasion is needed to change perception, and we place that responsibility squarely before our elected officials. (113)

MATTHEW COOPER'S "QUIT WORRYING"

The following two documents analyze a specific instance of race relations in the United States—the O.J. Simpson trial, during which he was accused but acquitted of the murder of his former wife, Nicole Brown Simpson, and her friend Ron Goldman. This trial is most frequently analyzed in terms of its racial component—a black defendant and two white victims—rather than a gendered or class distinction. Despite some feminists' attempts to keep the issue of domestic violence before the public, gender as a factor has dropped out of much of the conversation relating to the trial. And class (i.e., the fact that few Americans and very few African Americans could have afforded the degree of legal assistance that O.J. Simpson purchased) is commented on even less frequently. These details might indicate that Americans perceive race as a greater threat to social harmony than they do either gender or class.

Matthew Cooper, a journalist, argues that many people overreacted to the trial, not because it became a national obsession during the year it occurred but because, he predicts, it will have no lasting effect on race relations. Cooper maintains that individuals who suggest that a predominantly black jury would not convict a black man for murdering a white woman and a white man are ignoring a wealth of other information that suggests the contrary. He does not analyze the trial or the verdict as much as the culture's response to both. He implies that the event was an isolated one and that although differences in the perspectives of black and white Americans are undeniable, those differences do not suggest that the country is dramatically divided.

Cooper makes several references in his article that might be unfamiliar to you. The following descriptions should clarify any questions you might have. William Kennedy Smith is a member of the Kennedy family which includes President John F. Kennedy; he was accused of raping a woman at a family home in Florida. An Outward Bound experience is an adventure trip, generally including challenging physical tasks, designed to increase the confidence of participants. Mark Fuhrman was a member of the Los Angeles Police Department; his testimony damaged the prosecution's case in the Simpson trial because he appeared to be a blatant racist and many people believed he was capable of planting evidence against Simpson. The reference to Waco, Texas, alludes to the organization headed by David Koresh; many of his followers were killed there, and some Americans questioned the government's judgment in handling the case so aggressively. Similarly, a woman and child were killed at Ruby Ridge, Idaho, during a standoff between residents and members of the FBI; several members of Congress accused the FBI of handling the case poorly. Colin Powell was one of the most significant leaders of American forces during the Gulf War, and he is often pointed to as a possible candidate for national elected office. The statement about the space shuttle explosion refers to a disaster that occurred in 1986 when the space shuttle *Challenger* exploded shortly after liftoff. Among the crew members was Christa McAuliffe, a teacher. Grenada is a nation in the Caribbean; in 1983 the United States invaded the country in order establish a more democratic government. Finally, the Clarence Thomas–Anita Hill hearings were a series of events preceding Thomas's appointment to the U.S. Supreme Court. Anita Hill accused him of sexual harassment.

MATTHEW COOPER, "QUIT WORRYING"
(*The New Republic*, October 23, 1995)

In 1991, at the end of the Gulf war, I started to write but never finished a longish piece on how the conflict in the Persian Gulf might change America. The lightning-quick victory over Iraq, I thought, would lead to a celebration of what government could do. With faith restored in the public sector, liberals could cheer George Bush's war. I went even further: blacks and women would, I argued, demand their due back home after their sacrifice in the Gulf, sparking an era of activism not unlike the years following World War I and World War II when the suffrage and civil-rights movements got a boost.

The piece never ran, and boy am I glad it didn't. I was spectacularly wrong; the Gulf war seems to have had no lasting effect on the body politic. I suspect the same will be true of the Simpson verdict.

The same pundits who said the Simpson jury would take weeks to deliberate are now lamenting that the trial was a signal event in American race relations—exposing cleavages and exacerbating them. Perhaps. Yes, blacks and whites tended to see this case differently. They see a lot of things differently; just look at political-party affiliation or who watches what TV shows. But it's important to remember that from day to day, those differences tug on the country but they don't tear it. When it comes to courts, arguably the area of American life where the black and white gulf is at its widest, African Americans vote to convict African Americans all the time.

The charge that the jury system—and, indeed, the country—is infected by some kind of unhealthy tribalism is exaggerated. The Simpson verdict says less about a new racial divide and more about the longtime habits of jurors, black and white, who regularly fail to convict people who either appear, or in fact are, guilty. It shouldn't unduly surprise or dismay us that O.J. Simpson, like William Kennedy Smith, walks freely among us. A few weeks ago this magazine pointed to Los Angeles's twentysomethings as proof that the country was not descending into a multicultural abyss. . . . Such a cautionary note is worth remembering now that L.A. is being portrayed as a city divided.

Critics of Simpson's trial have pointed to the jury's hasty deliberations as proof of the lunacy of this verdict. Please. If the jury had decided in a matter of hours to *convict* Simpson, the very same people now decrying the speed of the verdict would be applauding the jury's decisiveness. The fact is that the jurors, like the rest of us, made up their minds a while ago, despite the hopelessly unrealistic judicial admonition not to form any opinions. This let-your-mind-go-totally-blank instruction never works when I've tried to meditate; it seems especially absurd when you figure these poor jurors have had to endure the ultimate Outward Bound experience. For more than a year they've been stuck in a time capsule, with nothing else to do but ponder the evidence. No wonder they decided quickly.

Are there sensible jury reforms to be enacted as a result of this case? Sure. Sequestration will hopefully fade from the legal scene like yesteryear's powdered wigs. Isolation in a modern society really is cruel and unusual punishment; and the proof that exposure to "publicity" will sway a juror one way or another seems dubious. It probably would have been better if, as some observers claim, the jury could have been more engaged, asking questions of the lawyers, talking among themselves. But the biggest reforms ought to be aimed at the police, not juries. That Mark Fuhrman should have been banished from the LAPD [Los Angeles Police Department] is, by now, a cliche; what's less remarked upon is that rogue cops seem to have insinuated themselves into too many American police forces. Philadelphia's police department, for one, has had to throw out dozens of cases after it emerged that police had set up victims and fabricated evidence.

The sloppiness and malevolence of such police work, decried by this magazine and others in the case of Waco, is fuel for the paranoids among us. Hatred of law enforcement is now a rallying cry on the left and right. The Ruby Ridge Republicans can't get enough of FBI and ATF [Bureau of Alcohol, Tobacco, & Firearms] bashing; black leaders direct their ire toward local police forces. Such wholesale suspicion of government is disheartening. But neither is it so unjustified or so widespread that it's worth despairing. Remember that as the O.J. verdict was read the most popular man in the country was an African American retired general. If suspicion of men in uniform dominated the landscape, if tribalism were out of control, then there would be no national hero called Colin Powell.

During mega-dramas such as the Simpson trial, conjecture and symbolmongering are irresistible, inevitable. The space shuttle explosion was dubbed a loss of innocence; the Grenada invasion was supposed to usher in a new era of American confidence; the Clarence Thomas–Anita Hill hearings were going to spark a generation of feminist activism. But in a complex culture no one event can be so defining because we're always on to the next. The Simpson verdict—rendered, after all, by blacks, whites and a Hispanic—may have been wrong, but neither is it cause for woeful handwringing. It's the converse of the famed Baby Jessica case, when a girl slipped down a Texas well and the nation was riveted by her rescue. That event, albeit smaller in scope, supposedly united the country just as Simpson's trial supposedly divides it. Neither is true. Both are mere moments in a country that is a paradox: divided and yet, mercifully, very much whole. (12)

JONETTA ROSE BARRAS'S "MY RACE, MY GENDER"

Much of the discussion of the O.J. Simpson trial assumes only two mutually exclusive choices—either Simpson committed the murders, or the Los Angeles police committed crimes such as planting evidence during their investigation. Of course, other choices are possible; for example, Simpson might be guilty, *and* the Los Angeles police department might have engaged in unethical and illegal practices. According to the American criminal justice system, however, criminal defendants must be convicted beyond a reasonable doubt; as long as sufficient doubt existed regarding the Los Angeles police department (or any other aspect of the prosecution's case), Simpson should have been acquitted (i.e., found not guilty).

Jonetta Rose Barras, an associate editor of *The Washington City Paper*, reveals her suspicion that Simpson is guilty and that he is not an admirable man despite his undeniable athletic talent. On the other hand, she acknowledges that this case does not exist in isolation—that even if it does not have a lasting effect on American race relations (as Matthew Cooper argues in the previous document), it does exist within a historical context. Because of specific cases throughout American history that illustrate dramatic miscarriages of justice, many Americans are suspicious when black men are accused of committing crimes against white women. As the women acknowledge in *A Raisin in the Sun*, the greatest fear of white Americans is not that African Americans will revert to an African stereotype and practice cannibalism, but that if integration is successful then black men will begin marrying white women. After describing situations in which police departments continue to abuse their power, Barras suggests that such historical facts of racial injustice persist in influencing contemporary criminal trials.

JONETTA ROSE BARRAS, "MY RACE, MY GENDER"
(*The New Republic*, October 25, 1995)

Back in the '70s, when I was a community organizer in Maryland, I met the cold face of the Prince George's County police. I had run through a stop sign—a simple enough infraction, you might think, but as a result, I had been brought to the Mt. Rainier station for questioning. After a few minutes of badgering by the white cops, I quickly remembered what I'd learned years ago in Mississippi: I spoke only when I was asked a direct question and was sure to punctuate each response with "sir." Just a few weeks before, a man named Terrence Johnson had been arrested and beaten only a mile from where I was detained. When I walked away with my health and a mere citation, I considered myself extremely lucky.

Go to any neighborhood where African Americans and Hispanics live, and you will find carbon copies of my story by the score. There is a common experience of being wrongly accused, of being beaten on "G.P." (general principal [*sic*]) that binds together African Americans, especially those who lived through the days of Jim Crow laws. This history and memory have been passed down from generation to generation as family folklore, early lessons taught again and again.

Johnnie L. Cochran, the lead attorney for the Orenthal James Simpson defense team, understood that the legacy of mistreatment by the American judicial system cannot be fully divested from the individual or collective black psyche. Even before Simpson's murder trial got under way, Cochran and the "Dream Team" unabashedly telegraphed their strategy. If necessary they would play their trump—the Race Card. Given the L.A. police force's record of corruption, Cochran knew he could beat a full house.

O.J. Simpson was no hero for me. I don't rent Hertz cars. I hate football, never saw him run one of his famous and remarkable touchdowns and don't much care that he's in the Hall of Fame. That he was crossover king—a black man so successful in a white world that he and others forgot his ghetto beginning—is irrelevant; there are others like him. I am particularly appalled and greatly offended by his consistent abuse of women. First he abandoned his wife for an affair with a white girl nearly young enough to be his daughter. Then, after finally placing a wedding ring on her finger and fathering children with her, he pounds on her—

more than once—as if she were a punching bag in his gym. His treatment of women alone made me ready to slap a guilty verdict across his chest.

But while the evidence seemed overwhelming in the beginning, Cochran and the defense team were effective at planting doubt: Was the DNA evidence properly handled? Was the crime scene contaminated? What was the exact time of death? The weapon remained elusive and an eye-witness was absent; the prosecution's case unraveled under the intensive scrutiny of the defense attorneys, particularly Barry Scheck and F. Lee Bailey. But it was the tape recordings of a bragging racist that opened a hole in the prosecution's case the size of a Mack truck, that made the defense's case, even for a majority female jury.

And it was those Mark Fuhrman tapes, more than anything else, that allowed justice to escape from the Los Angeles Courthouse last week. The jury learned that Fuhrman perjured himself when he testified that he had never used the word "nigger" to refer to an African American. Perhaps even more devastating were the reports of his loathing for interracial couples and his remark that, given the opportunity, he might even plant evidence, hoping to charge them with a crime. This was salt in an old, unhealed wound.

Gone from the minds of the majority female and black jury were issues of spousal abuse; gone were the scenes of an obsessive and possessive, rejected husband who became enraged at the sight of his ex-wife in another man's arms. Gone were the questions about whether he did or didn't have time to commit the crime and still make his flight to Chicago. Like an amnesiac flashing back to a former life, the O.J. Simpson jury recalled with remote accuracy the pain of a people too often accused of crimes they had not committed. Cochran subtly raised the specter of Emmett Till—the young black boy brutally mutilated, killed and then drowned for talking with a young white girl. He reminded the jury about the Scottsboro Boys—the black Alabamans falsely accused of rape by two white women. He invoked the beating of Rodney King. These stories are compelling and tangible parables about the derailing of justice for black men in America. And while the female jurors may have been angered by Simpson's treatment of women, there is no stronger thread than race in America; no mightier discord than racism. The jury became deaf to closing arguments; their minds were made up. Simpson was just another African American male caught in the snares of the system.

I was sure that the result of Fuhrman's display of venom would be a hung jury. But it gave me pause—and hope—when the jury asked to review the testimony of the limousine driver, who had arrived at Simpson's house the night of the murder. Although he twice telephoned for Simpson, the driver said he did not receive an answer. He reported seeing a black man matching the former football great's weight and height entering the house; just moments after, Simpson finally answered his phone. I thought perhaps the public might witness a rare show of courage; I thought color-blind justice might actually be served in Los Angeles. But this was only the wishful thinking of someone longing to move past the pain and start anew.

In the end, racism proved, once again, the most powerful force in America. The system stands indicted. While this time a black man was not found guilty, for me, he does not walk away innocent. (16)

EARL OFARI HUTCHINSON'S *BLACK FATHERHOOD*

The next two excerpts address the issue of alcohol abuse. Earl Ofari Hutchinson, an African-American writer who considers his audience to be other African Americans, expresses concern regarding the extent of alcohol and tobacco use among African Americans today, particularly young African Americans. He attributes this in part to the amount of advertising devoted to alcohol and tobacco in African American neighborhoods. His implicit question is why other less destructive products are not also advertised there. Within this scenario, a man like Walter Lee Younger would find himself in a double bind. To achieve his own independence he can own a business, but one of the few businesses he can expect to own is a liquor store. Yet abuse of and addiction to alcohol (as well as to tobacco and illegal drugs) would keep his African American customers from achieving their own independence. For even if African American alcoholics or drug addicts are not dependent on white employers for an income, no addict can be said to be truly free.

FROM EARL OFARI HUTCHINSON, *BLACK FATHERHOOD: THE GUIDE TO MALE PARENTING*
(Middle Passage Press, 1995)

Drive through any black neighborhood, and what do you see advertised on the billboards and bus stops? What are the main products sold in the stores there? Alcohol and tobacco. They do not get the publicity of hard drugs. They are not part of major national campaigns or crusades. They do not spread panic in communities.

Yet alcohol and tobacco are far more deadly to African-Americans. Each year they claim more black lives than hard drugs.

When America's liquor bill is totaled, blacks will pay more than twelve billion dollars. They will buy nearly one-third of the Scotch Whiskey sold in the country. One in five blacks is alcohol addicted. Three out of five young blacks drink.

If they drink, they are likely to smoke. African-Americans will buy triple the number of cigarettes that whites buy. They are twice as likely to die from lung cancer, emphysema and other respiratory ailments as whites. At least hard drugs are illegal; alcohol and tobacco aren't. (34)

STEVE OLSON'S *ALCOHOL IN AMERICA*

In this passage Steve Olson, an expert on alcohol abuse, addresses the effects of alcohol advertising. The point of any advertising, of course, is to encourage consumers to consume more. However, when a potentially destructive substance such as alcohol is advertised in the same way as a comparatively innocuous substance such as clothing or soft drinks, consumers are discouraged from considering the potential harm of the former. To the extent that Hutchinson is correct (see previous document) in stating that alcohol is over-advertised in African American neighborhoods, African Americans would suffer greater exploitation from this advertising than would other groups. Of course, it is difficult to measure precisely the specific effects of advertising, but corporations that spend millions of dollars per year on advertising clearly believe it works.

FROM STEVE OLSON IN COLLABORATION WITH DEAN R. GERSTEIN, *ALCOHOL IN AMERICA: TAKING ACTION TO PREVENT ABUSE* (National Academy Press, 1985)

The marketing of alcoholic beverages today is virtually indistinguishable from that of other products. Ads for alcoholic beverages are well researched, slickly produced, and backed by well-organized promotions at the retail level. Though the number of major brewers is dwindling, brands of beer are proliferating, many with their own advertising themes. . . .

A good example of the new emphasis on marketing was the Coca-Cola Company's effect on the wine market. When Coca-Cola bought the Taylor brand of wine in the late 1970s, it set out to promote the image of wine as a drink that is consumed regularly rather than just on special occasions. Within a few years the amount of advertising in the wine industry nearly doubled—largely because of Coca-Cola's aggressive marketing techniques.

The tactics used to advertise alcohol differ little from those used with other products. Advertisements may indirectly associate drinking with wealth, success, or social approval. They may portray drinking as a sexy, sophisticated act. . . .

The effect of such advertising remains a point of controversy. Researchers have never been able to agree on whether alcohol advertising increases the amount people drink or simply influences what brand of alcohol they buy. . . .

The National Research Council panel on alcohol abuse has also decided that the jury is still out on the influence of alcohol advertising. "It is generally thought that the main effect of commercial advertising is to alert the public to new brands, in competition with older ones, and conversely to protect or expand the market shares of established brands," the panel concludes. "The available scientific evidence is too sparse to permit us any extended discussion of the effects of advertising policies. Nevertheless, important issues of principle are involved in such policies." (85–86)

H. EDWARD RANSFORD'S *RACE AND CLASS*

The next several excerpts focus on education. Clearly, ideas about education play a major role in *A Raisin in the Sun*. Not only does Beneatha aspire to several years of rigorous higher education in her dream to become a doctor, but it is through an educational institution—her college—that she has met Asagai, who introduces her to a more positive interpretation of her ancestry and cultural heritage.

In this excerpt H. Edward Ransford, a researcher on race and education, discusses the fact that today's lower-class black children remain at greatest risk for educational failure. Although some researchers may attribute this failure rate to the children's environment (e.g., lack of books in the home), Ransford suggests that another explanation may lie in the system itself. To the extent that a middle-class white child's style of achievement is adopted as a standard, children who do not fit that standard will be more inclined to fail regardless of the particular arena in which success is measured. Ransford's suggestion is that modes of instruction need to be altered to match the diverse backgrounds of all American children.

FROM H. EDWARD RANSFORD, *RACE AND CLASS IN AMERICAN*
SOCIETY: BLACK, LATINO, ANGLO
(Schenkman Books, 1994)

Lower-class black and Latino children are far more likely to drop out of school and fall further behind at each grade level in their achievements than middle-class white, middle-class black, and middle-class Latino children. Unfortunately, the most common explanation for failure has been the lower-class minority environment or the "cultural deprivation" or "culture of poverty" explanation. . . . [T]his explanation asserts that components of a depressed environment—apathy, low motivation, lack of cognitive interaction between parents and children, and a lack of books and magazines—cause failure. . . .

It is only recently that educational institutions themselves, their policies and their programs, have been studied in any critical, systematic way in this regard. In this literature, one finds articles on teacher expectations for failure, abuse in the use of IQ tests in classifying lower-class black and Chicano children, the negative consequences of tracking, and the class-ethnic composition of the student body as the determiner of "cooling out" mechanisms. The study of the patterns of racism and classism in educational institutions is an extremely important area with obvious implications for policy research. The failure to educate lower-class black and Latino children is seen by many as not so much a function of a depressed environment as of an insensitive reaction of educational institutions to children produced from this environment—that is, the mechanical tendency to sort and classify students according to the degree to which they match the middle-class Anglo model. Schools are not so much deliberately attempting to exclude lower-class minority children as they are perpetuating an impersonal "conveyer belt" of failure for them by favoring an unmodified adherence to middle-class Anglo standards. There is often total insensitivity to the background of the lower-class child. (176–77)

HILLARY RODHAM CLINTON'S *IT TAKES A VILLAGE*

In this book, First Lady Hillary Rodham Clinton relies on the expression "It takes a village to raise a child" to express her belief that children are influenced by many more people than their parents or other immediate relatives. According to Clinton, all members of a community, whether it is defined locally or nationally, must assume some responsibility for that community's children. In this excerpt Clinton address the debate over "nature" and "nurture." Proponents of "nature" argue that children are either born with talent or born without it, and that children born without talent are destined to fail regardless of the help they are given. Children born with talent will succeed, on the other hand, even if they are given no help at all. Thus, these people argue, investing in schools is a waste of money. Clinton points to evidence that this is not true—that much success depends on "nurture," that is, on a child's environment and on the events that occur in a child's life after birth. Americans, she claims, attribute too much to nature and, therefore, too often fail to assume responsibility for nurture.

FROM HILLARY RODHAM CLINTON, *IT TAKES A VILLAGE AND OTHER LESSONS CHILDREN TEACH US*
(Simon and Schuster, 1996)

The main point I want to make here is that virtually all children can learn and develop more than their parents, teachers, or the rest of the village often believe. This has great implications for how we approach our children's educations.

One of the striking differences international studies have repeatedly turned up between American parents and students and their counterparts in other countries . . . is the greater weight our culture currently gives to innate ability, as opposed to effort, in academic success. I don't know all the reasons for this preoccupation, which seems to be linked to an obsession with IQ tests and other means of labeling people, but some possible explanations are not particularly flattering to us.

Believing in innate ability is a handy excuse for us. . . .

The bell curve lets the rest of us off the hook too. What's the sense of reforming schools, especially if it costs any money? What is the point of figuring out how to tailor teaching to the unique ways children learn? Why puzzle over what they should learn, and why bother to articulate it to them? Cream will rise to the top no matter what we do, so let nature take its course and forget about nurture.

If we are permitted to write off whole groups of kids because of their racial or ethnic or economic backgrounds, then the occasional academic shooting star will be seen as a fluke. And when whole groups of kids succeed despite the odds, like the poor Hispanic high school students Jaime Escalante coached to succeed on the Advanced Placement calculus examination, their success can be ascribed to a unique brand of charismatic teaching and motivation that can't be replicated anywhere else. (243–44)

TAHISHA BERESFORD'S EXPERIENCE

The final two documents in this chapter are autobiographical accounts of African American college students. They address their experiences within the educational system and its relationship to their professional goals.

Tahisha Beresford was born in Brooklyn, New York. In the 1990s she is a first-year college student studying culinary arts. In her essay she acknowledges that she has experienced racism but that so far it has not influenced her professional life. She has not felt compelled to choose a certain career simply because some options were closed to her. Indicating that progress has occurred in the area of race relations, she argues that success primarily depends on a person's own assumption of responsibility.

TAHISHA BERESFORD, "IT'S NOT ALWAYS ABOUT THE COLOR
OF YOUR SKIN"
(1997)

Being an African American woman growing up in the 1990s has not affected my career goals in the least. As long as I have a good head on my shoulders and a proper education, I can be anything or go anywhere I want to in life. Being an African American has not in any way hindered me from growing in my field of business. I am always treated with the respect that I deserve. I am treated as an individual person based on my character.

I'm not saying that there has never been a time when I was called a "Nigger" or had someone swear at me, but it was never in the work place. It wasn't because I'm an African American, and it was never said to offend me, although it did.

Growing up in the 1990s, I have more freedom, a voice, and a right to vote, unlike my ancestors. I have a choice, and I have a say about issues that surround me. I have more and better opportunities in the 1990s than my ancestors did some 439 years ago. Whether I am African American or not, my life is what I make of it. I'm not saying that race will never play a part in the work place, in life, or any field of business. I know that discrimination has happened to some people just because of their race or gender, but it has never happened to me. If a person is well equipped, has the intellectual status required to work in a certain business, is well rounded, and puts God before every person and everything, he or she cannot be stopped.

Often times, African Americans will blame Caucasians for their troubles. That excuse is no longer relevant in the 1990s; it would have been 439 years ago. But now that African Americans have the same rights as any other race in the United States, blaming Caucasians is nothing more than a mere cop-out. African Americans no longer have to read in secret or be taught by the master's wife when the master isn't home, nor are African Americans not allowed to get a good education. The opportunities are right there; it's what you do with them that determines where you stand in life.

I will take advantage of every opportunity that comes my way because I want to be all that I can be. I am not going to let my race or my gender stop me from becoming what I want to be. Education is for everyone, but it is the one who takes advantage of it who will succeed in life.

SAMANTHA DAY'S EXPERIENCE

Samantha Day is a second-year college student studying nursing in the 1990s. She was born in Far Rockaway, Queens, New York, and attended Clara Barton High School in Brooklyn, New York, where she also studied nursing. In her essay she states that she has experienced incidents of racism as a student, which she attributes in part to her choice of a profession. Because health-care workers have traditionally been white, she suggests that many Americans expect their doctors and nurses to be white and express overt or subtle racism when they are cared for by African Americans. She suggests that statements that do not seem to be racialized (e.g., "Perhaps nursing isn't for you") might be the result of discrimination. She reveals the complexity of race relations in America by stating that some white people feel they must go out of their way to demonstrate that they are *not* racist. She describes this behavior as "discouraging" because it indicates that people seldom respond to each other "naturally," that is, without being aware of one another's race.

SAMANTHA DAY, "MY NURSING EXPERIENCE"
(1997)

African-Americans have struggled for equality and justice for years and years. Civil rights leaders have fought for the human rights that were once denied to Blacks by the American culture. African-Americans were seen as an inferior culture who were good for nothing but cleaning, cooking, and attending to the needs of the superior White race.

Women have also had to fight for the right to be equal. Women were only valued for their ability to bear children and maintain a household. It took many strong women in history to bring forth the semi-equality that is present now.

The medical field in itself is a difficult and demanding field to enter. It is challenging and biased against people who are not seen as the typical nurse or doctor. The ideal health care provider is usually pictured as a clean-cut, older, white man as a doctor, with a young, white, female as the nurse.

Therefore, as both an African American and a woman entering the health care field, I have had to fight plenty of battles of my own and overcome plenty of negative attitudes to reach my dream of becoming a nurse.

Although America would like to believe that racism is an issue of the past, I definitely believe that racism exists now as much as it may have in the days of *A Raisin in the Sun*. In those times, the character of Beneatha was discouraged by her family and others from becoming a doctor because it "wasn't accepted." Currently, society continues not to accept African Americans in the medical field, but their belief is overshadowed by what the government would call "ethics." Everyone is *supposed* to be treated equally and is, therefore, provided with "equal opportunities."

In my opinion, I was provided with the opportunity of becoming a nurse, although I am not treated equally. Unlike some members of Beneatha's family, my family strongly supports my career decision. My family praises me for all the hard work and dedication that they see me devoting to this nursing program. Unfortunately, my family is the only real support that I have. The main barriers I feel in my struggle to achieve my career choice are the people who provide me with my education. I've learned not to look for all of my professors to offer a reassuring or helpful hand. For example, there have been times I would approach my professors for help, and instead they would try to discourage me and say things like, "Maybe nursing just isn't for you." I have also been in situations where my professors would make jokes about my culture and biased statements such as "you people are all the same," or "you were probably listening to all that rap music instead of studying!" It is also discouraging when some of my professors act too nicely because they feel sorry for me, or they want to show that they are not prejudiced. I believe that the reason some of my professors act this way is because many of them were raised in the times when racism was accepted and in some households encouraged.

I have also encountered racial attitudes and stereotypes from my classmates. Ninety-nine percent of my classmates are white, and are fulfilling society's perceptions of good health care providers. Although studying nursing is very competitive, there is unity in the nursing program. Unfortunately, the unity is not multicultural; all students of the same race stick together and compete against the three black students that remain in the program.

With all the barriers that are faced in the medical field, one might wonder, Why do it? Well, I feel that if I give up, the people who were against me would achieve their goal and those who encouraged me, as well as myself, would be disappointed. I feel like the struggles that people in the past had to go through would be in vain. Therefore, I continue to reach for the stars that my culture has been deprived of for so many years.

TOPICS FOR WRITTEN OR ORAL EXPLORATION

1. Analyze Mama's resistance to Walter's business goals. Do you believe Mama would have been more willing to give him money if he had intended to open a different kind of business?

2. Analyze the scene in which Walter is drunk. What are his motives for drinking? In what ways is his behavior in this scene consistent or inconsistent with his behavior in other scenes?

3. Compare and contrast Beneatha's attitude toward education with George's. What do they believe the goals and purposes of education are? How do these beliefs affect the type of education they seek?

4. Write a story or play featuring the characters in *A Raisin in the Sun* but set in a more contemporary period. Consider not only how society has changed, but also how you believe the characters would have grown and changed as they aged.

5. Choose a corporation or local business and research its racial policies concerning personnel. Consider not only who is employed but at what level they are employed.

6. Discuss the ethical questions that might arise for individuals who desire to start a business. Consider whether owners of liquor stores or bars have responsibilities that other businesspeople do not.

7. Watch a movie or television program, noting the references to alcohol or the occasions when characters drink. Discuss how alcohol is represented in the mass media.

8. Write an essay describing your own educational and professional goals. Include a plan for the next five years of your life.

9. Write a research paper on a recent local or national incident in which race played a major role. Analyze the coverage given to this event in various publications.

10. Write a paper offering a solution to a particular racial conflict in your school or community.

11. After reading the articles about alcohol use, write a response to Hutchinson or Olson. Are their perceptions about the presence of alcohol in the mass media similar to your own?

12. Write an essay in which you address the distinction between innate ability and effort described by Hillary Rodham Clinton. Discuss an occasion when you experienced success. Do you believe your success occurred primarily because of raw talent or of effort? Do you believe your experience is similar to or different from the experience of most of your classmates?

SUGGESTED READINGS

Astin, Alexander W. *Minorities in Higher Education*. San Francisco: Jossey-Bass, 1988.

Byrnes, Tom, et al. *Madam Foreman: A Rush to Judgment?* Los Angeles: Dove, 1995.

Darden, Christopher. *In Contempt*. New York: HarperCollins, 1996.

Dershowitz, Alan. *Reasonable Doubt: The O.J. Simpson Case and the Criminal Justice System*. New York: Simon and Schuster, 1996.

Morrison, Toni, and Claudia Brodsky Lacour, eds. *Birth of a Nation 'Hood: Gaze, Script and Spectacle in the O.J. Simpson Case*. New York: Pantheon, 1997.

Patterson, Orlando. *The Ordeal of Integration: Progress and Resentment in America's "Racial" Crisis*. Washington, DC: Civitas Counterpoint, 1997.

Shipler, David. *A Country of Strangers: Blacks and Whites in America*. New York: Alfred A. Knopf, 1997.

Index

About the Author

LYNN DOMINA is Assistant Professor in the Department of Humanities, Social Science, and Individual Studies at SUNY–Delhi. She has published articles on Zora Neale Hurston, Mary McCarthy, N. Scott Momaday, and others. Her first book of poetry, *Corporal Works*, was published in 1995.

Edwards Brothers, Inc.
Thorofare, NJ USA
November 10, 2011